D1599761

ELEVATION

116-18567 1 OF 5 SHEETS

·UNION·PASSENGER·STATION·
·KANSAS·CITY·MO·
·JARVIS·HUNT·ARCHITECT·CHICAGO·

DEC.1ST 1910

10

Still Standing

Still

RAILROADS PAST AND PRESENT

George M. Smerk, editor

INDIANA UNIVERSITY PRESS • *Bloomington and Indianapolis*

Standing

A Century of Urban Train Station Design

Christopher Brown

All photographs in this book are by Christopher Brown, with the
exception of the 1893 World's Columbian Exposition photograph on
page 4, which appears courtesy of the Chicago Historical Society.

This book is a publication of

Indiana University Press
601 North Morton Street
Bloomington, IN 47404-3797 USA

http://iupress.indiana.edu

Telephone orders   800-842-6796
Fax orders   812-855-7931
Orders by e-mail   iuporder@indiana.edu

The paper used in this publication meets the minimum requirements of
American National Standard for Information Sciences—Permanence
of Paper for Printed Library Materials, ANSI Z39.48-1984.

Manufactured in China

Library of Congress Cataloging-in-Publication Data

Brown, Christopher, date-
  Still standing : a century of urban train station design / Christopher Brown.
      p. cm. – (Railroads past and present)
  Includes bibliographical references and index.
  ISBN 0-253-34634-7 (cloth : alk. paper)
  1. Railroad stations—History. I. Title. II. Series.
  TF300.B76 2005
  725'.31—dc22
                                             2004029965

1 2 3 4 5 10 09 08 07 06 05

Facing page: The rotunda at Cincinnati's Union Terminal.

To Michael Peretzian

Make no little plans. They have no magic to stir men's blood.

—DANIEL H. BURNHAM

Contents

Preface

I remember as a very young boy traveling by train with my mother from my small hometown to that strange and alien place I knew simply as "the city," a locale so foreign to me yet even then so filled with questions and possibilities. As we neared our destination, the rolling wooded hills gave way to a flatter, not so tidy grid of towns and the acrid smell of factories. The mundane sights and sounds that moved ever slower past my train car window went almost unobserved as I focused on what was up ahead around the corner as only a child can. We must be getting closer.

As we stepped down from our train onto the platform, a river of passengers flowed in only one direction to the stairs, up to larger spaces ever more grand than the ones before, until there we were—entering the main concourse of a magnificent urban train station. It was huge and beautiful as light streamed into the room in a way I'd seen only in photographs. The giant chandeliers were bigger than my family's car. The footsteps of a thousand visitors on the burnished marble were soft. That white noise wrapped around me like my favorite blanket.

One's childhood experiences perhaps do little to explain an interest in these splendid buildings, especially to those not like-minded. For me, the experience is about the sense of enclosure of the space itself and the embrace and comfort it provides. It's about the act of looking upward. I liken the experience to that of an individual who visits a few too many cathedrals during a cultural tour of Europe. "If you've seen one . . ." But of course the tour of cathedrals is about more than the physicality of the space. The visitor taps into a sense of something larger. In short, the visit is charged.

A visit to many of the great stations of the world is charged for me as well. Not spiritually, mind you, but charged as in a great theatrical experience—the station as a proscenium arch, the stage for all forms of human emotion, those actions, words, and tears which were somewhat removed and foreign to me in my own childhood.

How do I begin to explain the lump in my throat I have often experienced when first entering some of the magnificent stations included in this volume? Well, in a sense, I hear voices and I see ghosts. Sometimes it's the image of a young GI saying good-bye to his best gal before shipping off to the South Pacific; at times it's the image of a newly arrived immigrant dazzled by the grand surroundings en route to a teeming urban neighborhood not much different from the one he left behind. Sometimes I see the glimmer of an artisan high on a scaffold adding his deft touch to this, a precious monument to an era gone by. I can see the value he places in his own craft and in an honest day's work. But more likely than not I see that young boy, my former self, with eyes lifted upward. The railroad station taught him by example how to live and to love; to mourn the separation from a loved one and to anxiously anticipate that reunion just around the pillar. The station always provided a privileged glimpse of common humanity from which he was carefully shielded but never far removed.

The big city station continued to teach me into adulthood, and my visits persisted long after the flow of the trains and the crowds had slowed to a trickle. I often think of that young boy, about those lessons learned at an early age. How fortunate he was to have experienced the awe and theater of the train station in full bloom. Does it matter that this experience has virtually vanished in America? Does it matter that it's gone? Perhaps not, but I remember.

The pristine former Harvey House restaurant at Los Angeles Union Station.

Introduction

What a luxury it is to examine an art form that is seemingly finite in nature! One naively hopes that a "through line" of design can be easily uncovered while examining a specific time frame. Yet a complex combination of factors, such as local climate, site topography, technical innovations, corporate ego, notions of national identity, and regional aesthetics, often conspired to twist and contort any linear development of the train station form that might have otherwise occurred.

Train stations were first built in England in the 1820s. As popularity and dependency on passenger train travel grew, architects and engineers were asked to coordinate the movement and accommodation of great numbers of people with the movement and accommodation of large machines. Railroading was a new invention, and a new kind of structure would have to be created to house it. The form was not immediately apparent, and there were no models in Western culture for buildings that served society in quite this way.

In his 1956 work *The Railroad Station*, Carroll Meeks, the unrivaled father of railroad station architectural history, found the process of architectural classification of station design so unwieldy that he defined a new aesthetic, a means of categorizing three distinct but unified periods of station evolution between 1830 and 1914. What appeared to others as a series of unrelated nineteenth-century classical revivals was unified by Meeks in his concept of Picturesque Eclecticism. The picturesque design, which stressed a varied asymmetrical silhouette using chimneys, towers, complex roof lines, and advancing and receding planes within a specific elevation, was partnered with an eclecticism defined by Meeks as the liberal borrowing from many styles in an attempt not only to be original but to emphasize the primary architectural style used in a specific composition.

The Basics

The world's earliest stations were *one-sided*, with all passenger and baggage facilities placed to one side of the active train tracks. As volume grew, arriving and departing passenger functions were split between opposite sides of the tracks for smoother pedestrian flow; these were referred to as *two-sided* stations. With volume ever increasing, the *head house station* evolved. A larger single structure was built combining all ancillary passenger functions and permitting the smooth mix of arriving and departing passengers under one roof.

The world's train stations fall into two basic categories that dictate their physical layout in relationship to the actual train tracks. *Through stations* were constructed on the side of tracks or between tracks on a through route. In the United States and much of the New World, a station's location often preceded the real growth of the city, thus permitting the construction of through stations. *Stub-end stations* are the most prevalent forms found in the major cities of Europe. The rise of the railroads occurred after these cities were already established. Stations were pushed to the outer fringe of the city's central core. Tracks came into the city and the station from one direction and stopped. This form of station facility offered an efficient design for passenger processing and required less real estate.

The History

In order to provide a base for examining the development of urban train station design, it would seem helpful to provide a brief history in broad strokes to accompany the visual tour to follow.

THE 1820S AND 1830S

As expected, most early stations were adapted from a previous use, whether it be an old storefront, a converted house, an inn, or a warehouse. As passenger numbers grew, these make-do spaces were altered to accommodate. Early stations in Britain built specifically for railroad purposes were usually wooden structures. Iron roofs made their first appearance at London Euston Station by 1839. Quite naturally the engineering of train sheds, those structures covering train tracks and platforms, progressed more rapidly wherever weather was most severe.

THE 1840S

The French and the English took different approaches to designing station head houses. A formal architectural education was already available in France. Early French station designs were dependent on formal architectural rules. Designers embraced the monumental while employing motives that expressed a station's internal function. English designers seemed more concerned with an aesthetic sense and borrowed liberally from any style for their station statements. The early adoption of classical styles in England had given way to an Italian Villa style that was used so frequently it became known as Railroad Style (see Connolly Station, Dublin, page 7).

THE 1850S

The look of stations in the United Kingdom and Europe was to be inordinately influenced by London's Crystal Palace of 1850. The newly mastered engineering feat of combining iron and glass to enclose and protect large spaces, as if constructing a giant greenhouse, was embraced by the railroads on both sides of the channel. When this form was adapted for station use, the height of the space allowed for the dissipation of acrid engine smoke and steam while offering passengers protection from the elements. In fact, the arch utilized in shed construction is often cited as the single most important design innovation of the entire nineteenth century (see Paddington Station, London, page 17). The development of the large train shed marked the beginning of an uneasy coexistence between shed engineer and head house architect that would continue into the twentieth century. The first examples of consolidating these two disparate elements, and an early attempt to answer the nagging architectural question of how form and function interrelate, can be seen in Paris and London around the same time that the arch of a train shed was expressed on the main facade of a head house (see Gare de l'Est, Paris, page 13). This use of the arch not only would become symbolic of the shed behind but also would serve as a symbol of the station as gateway to the city and an internationally understood signpost for any large train station. By extension this expressed arch would ultimately become a symbol of the railroads' might in the marketplace.

Although Americans were building stations during this period, often sizable barn-like structures that were fully self-contained, little of note was constructed. With great distances to cross and new cities growing, U.S. railroads concentrated on their spreading infrastructure before committing vast sums for substantial stations.

THE 1860S AND 1870S

Passenger loads continued to rise, and the race was on by the 1860s to stretch the limits of technology while striving for larger train shed enclosures and bigger single arch spans. The British and the French vied for bragging rights. In general, the French sheds appeared narrower and lighter in appearance than the sheds of the British Isles (see Gare du Nord, Paris, page 22). British engineers would continue to work toward a 3:1 width-to-height proportion as the aesthetic ideal. The Italian Villa style was replaced by Victorian Gothic architecture as the style of choice, especially in Britain (see St. Pancras Station, London, page 25). Formal waiting rooms were abandoned for a time, with new emphasis given to the station concourse or to cross platforms at the end of stub-end tracks for the ability to accommodate waiting passengers and mix the traffic flow of departing and arriving passengers. Lagging far behind the European station builders, Americans finally constructed a world-class train station in New York City.

THE 1880S

By the 1880s, Romanesque architecture, traceable to the Round Arch School of Germany, was in vogue. The style was reinvigorated by American architect H. H. Richardson. His heavy-handed yet satisfying take with broad, deep archways in dark, rough-hewn stone was substantial and widely embraced not only for train stations but also for civic buildings, large and small, across North America (see Dearborn Street Station, Chicago, page 35).

In Europe, architects were winning the informal competition between shed and head house as massive terminal buildings were being constructed often in a U shape, to front and enclose immense glazed sheds and obscure them from view (see Hauptbahnhof, Frankfurt-am-Main, page 37).

THE 1890S

The Richardsonian Romanesque architecture in North America began to morph, blending with other styles. The largest train sheds ever built were constructed during this period. Yet the American railroads'

devotion to the shed faltered as the shed shape began to move indoors, becoming part of the head house, while the actual sheds lacked a similar excitement. The reign of the balloon train shed, at least in North America, was coming to a close (see Union Station, St. Louis, page 44).

THE 1900S AND 1910S

As America strutted its stuff on the world stage, the construction and replacement of its urban terminals produced some of the largest and often most immoderate examples of train station architecture. The Beaux-Arts tenets popularized and advanced by Daniel H. Burnham were making their mark on the urban landscape. Station designs began to spread horizontally. Beaux-Arts was perfectly suited for the task (see Union Station, Washington, D.C., page 55, and Grand Central Terminal, New York City, page 73). Yet, as the skylines of American cities rose, so did a handful of urban train stations. *The station as office building* first appeared in Philadelphia at the very end of the nineteenth century, with additional examples popping up in Detroit and Pittsburgh, then later in Cleveland and Buffalo (see Pennsylvania Station, Pittsburgh, page 47).

The balloon shed died a quick death in the United States with the invention of the Bush shed in 1906, while in the same year Europe completed construction of its last great glazed train shed at Hamburg. Europe had completed construction of most of the important stations on the Continent by this time. In certain regions the popularity of Art Nouveau in art and architecture, coupled with a growing nationalistic bent that sometimes followed years of subjugation or preceded the growing threat of war, resulted in some interesting hybrid architecture (see Hlavani Station, Prague, page 65, and Rautatieasema, Helsinki, page 83).

Canadian railroads ignored the fine tradition of châteauesque station design and embraced Neoclassical design in most new station projects (see Vancouver Station, page 77, and Union Station, Toronto, page 91).

Several major fairs on the West Coast of the United States celebrating the completion of the Panama Canal generated new public interest in Latin America and, in turn, a rediscovery of Spanish Mission styles indigenous to the U.S. Southwest (see Santa Fe Depot, San Diego, page 79).

THE 1920S

Away and beyond in Australia and New Zealand, big-city stations were either built new or renovated following Renaissance or classical models, and this brought a handful of urban terminals up to par with their Northern Hemisphere contemporaries (see Railroad Station, Auckland, page 103).

The little construction that took place in Europe at this time was concentrated in France, where several midsize stations were built, leaning heavily on either a Norman provincial or a stripped classicism vernacular.

U.S. passenger rail traffic peaked in 1920, yet that fact seems unacknowledged by large American railroads. The reign of Beaux-Arts in North America would soon be over, but ground was broken for several megastations that further explored Neoclassical themes while retaining some of the stylistic cues of the École des Beaux-Arts (see Union Station, Chicago, page 95).

THE 1930S

In spite of the desperate economic climate worldwide, the first real twists in design could be seen since Beaux-Arts had raised its pompous head. A handful of high-profile station projects were completed despite the Depression, as trendy Art Deco and Art Moderne styles blended with stripped Neoclassicism (see Thirtieth Street Station, Philadelphia, page 107, and Union Terminal, Cincinnati, page 111).

In Europe, extreme shifts in contemporary design were in store. The Netherlands stepped forward as the idea lab in the 1930s for a developing Functionalism, also known at the time as International Style. Several midsize stations, embracing these Modernist concepts, were completed before Europe was plunged into war once again (see Santa Maria Novella Station, Florence, page 119).

THE 1940S AND 1950S

Reaction to the widespread damage and often total destruction of terminal facilities throughout Europe was overshadowed by more pressing reconstruction issues. Often devastated stations continued to serve a diminished passenger load without repairs well into the 1950s. Stations that could be restored were eventually given full attention, reflecting the vital importance of rail travel on the Continent. Those terminal facilities deemed beyond help were cleared away to make room for mediocre replacements like those found in Berlin and Munich. All too rare was the completion of a true Modernist statement that might compete visually with high-priced, privately funded commissions (see Termini Station, Rome, page 127).

In North America the final curtain was being lowered on passenger rail service, but no one really noticed. What was built was uninspired, often borrowing heavily from bus station architecture, as North Americans embraced their automobiles and never let go. True Modernist statements were too avant-garde for the conservative heads of this continent's struggling railroads.

THE 1960S

Although the visual survey to follow ends in the early 1950s, the last gasp of station design was really the 1960s, when some utterly bland large-scale projects were completed in the UK and Western Europe. Forced in some instances to build anew to serve a steady passenger base, the railroads of Europe did not have the dubious luxury of their North American counterparts. American and Canadian railroads could gesture mutely to dwindling passenger loads in justifying their own indifference toward their station facilities. And so it was that this great arc of urban train station design came sputtering to an end with the use of concrete slabs at London's second Euston Station in 1968 and Paris's Montparnasse in 1969.

Following a lengthy period of station neglect and destruction, and a worldwide struggle of state-run railroads to maintain service, the construction and reemergence in Europe of architecturally significant train stations was indeed a welcome shock. As population densities rose, coupled with the problems inherent in Europe's growing dependency on the automobile, a newfound enthusiasm for rapid train travel arrived. Starting in the early 1990s, breathtaking new terminals have been constructed primarily in Europe to serve both high-speed and traditional intercity train travel. The tradition of providing the traveling public with an awe-inspiring station experience is still alive. This next generation of railroad stations has been documented extensively in other volumes.

Daniel H. Burnham and the Emergence of Beaux-Arts Style

The arrival of Beaux-Arts Neoclassicism in the United States at the end of the nineteenth century had a profound and long-lasting effect on the design of larger public buildings throughout the country. Nowhere was the influence felt more than in the design of urban train stations. It was a style that in many ways was a perfect fit with America at the turn of the century. It was ostentatious in its presentation, inherently pretentious, monumental, and often just plain over the top. In short, it truly reflected a nation coming into its own. To this day, this specific variant based on classical models holds a special charm that has had the power to embarrass architectural critics and historians alike. The influence of Beaux-Arts style continued until the curtain of the Great Depression dropped on the world stage.

At a time in history when opportunities for the formal study of architecture were limited, many American students of the art studied at the École des Beaux-Arts in Paris. These architects returned home with a reverence for ancient Greek and Roman building styles blended with Renaissance motives, all interpreted in a grandiose way. Beaux-Arts as it was expressed in the United States was not so much a style as it was a manner of revisiting classical architectural models. In practice, architects peppered their designs with colossal columns and pilasters, various stone finishes, and the liberal use of exuberant Baroque detailing. The facade of a Beaux-Arts building was generally a symmetrical composition broken into advancing and receding planes, often featuring a central pavilion. Pronounced cornices and enriched entablatures were topped with tall parapets, balustrades, or monumental attic stories. All of this was often liberally embellished with lush decorative statuary. Borrowing solely from the past, architects working in this Beaux-Arts idiom sought beauty, not a new architectural language.

Daniel H. Burnham (1846–1912) ran a successful Chicago architectural firm in the 1870s and 1880s. His firm's signature structure was an early form of skyscraper. By most accounts Burnham was a man of contradictions. He was a shrewd businessman and socially ambitious, yet likable, kind to employees, and loyal to friends. As a technician, his greatest strength was his keen ability to plan a space based on a client's wants and needs. The exterior appearance and ornamentation of a completed commission was often an eclectic mix of styles and almost always the work of a strong but less visible partner back in the office.

In 1890 the city of Chicago won the support of Congress to move forward on a world's fair to commemorate the 400th anniversary of the discovery of America, to be called the Columbian Exposition. Daniel Burnham had spent many years courting the business leaders of Chicago who were greatly involved in the future of the fair. It is not surprising that he was named director of works as well as a consulting architect for the 1,000-acre site. He would ultimately run the show. Burnham and the expo's planning committee recommended the construction of an "architectural court," a series of individual but unified monumental theme buildings arranged around a large but formal body of water as a point of focus. It was agreed that the buildings of the court would be individually impressive but of a similar style. Burnham personally invited some of America's biggest names in the commercial design world to contribute and display their talents: Peabody & Stearns of Boston; Van Brunt & Howe of Kansas City; and Richard M. Hunt, George B. Post, and the firm of McKim, Mead & White, all of New York. Some of the architects resisted the invitation and required some subtle arm-twisting. Burnham promised as if he somehow knew that the completed "White City," as the court would later be known, would serve as a font of inspiration for American architecture and urban planning for years to come.

View across west end of the architectural court, World's Columbian Exposition, Chicago, 1893. Photographer unknown. Photo number LCHi-25057. Courtesy Chicago Historical Society.

In the closing years of the nineteenth century, the United States was growing quickly. Its burgeoning cities struggled to accommodate massive waves of immigrants. To those newcomers with a vivid memory of simple village life or urban squalor left behind, the experience of visiting the Columbian Exposition with its glimmering white monumental buildings could only have been overwhelming. For five months in mid-1893, the exposition's White City *became* America.

The arrival and popular embrace of Beaux-Arts in the United States can easily be traced to Chicago's Columbian Exposition. How it manifested itself there is not as easy to ascertain. It seems quite possible Daniel Burnham held no specific architectural agenda when initially planning the White City. What he did do consciously was to provide a platform, a blank canvas for accomplished artists. In the end, Burnham had successfully orchestrated the construction and completion of one of the most overwhelming and impressive collections of Beaux-Arts Neoclassicism built on any single plot in the world, and the nation took notice. The Columbian Exposition was a major national cultural event of the nineteenth century and captured the imagination of Americans from all corners of the continent.

Burnham & Co. continued to function as a highly successful architectural firm practicing a form of Beaux-Arts Neoclassicism sometimes referred to dismissively as "commercial classicism" or more pointedly as "Burnham Baroque." Daniel Burnham understood the *business* of architecture while embracing in his later years a popular but critically disregarded architectural style.

The man largely responsible for the promotion and popular embrace of Beaux-Arts Neoclassicism in North America has virtually escaped his due praise. The twentieth century witnessed a backlash and generally negative reaction to the preponderance of Beaux-Arts in the United States as the building style of choice for larger projects. Famed Chicago architect Louis Sullivan, a professional friend of Burnham and design participant in the Columbian Expo, took a broad swing at what he saw as harm done to the nation's urban landscape by the fair's architecture. Sullivan waited until 1924 to take the swing, but swing he did, saying, "The damage wrought by the World's Fair will last for half a century." Still others have complained of trend-conscious American architects of the day who were jumping on the Beaux-Arts bandwagon, resulting in "a proliferation of eclectic mediocrity" (Hines, *Burnham of Chicago*, 46). Even Burnham biographer Thomas Hines tends to discount any cultural value Beaux-Arts may hold, stating, "However justified and appropriate it may have seemed at the time, the 'classical' White City and the 'classical' revival that it introduced were retrograde forces in American culture" (ibid., 123). More than 100 years have passed since Beaux-Arts debuted in the United States, and disapproval of the form is still somewhat palpable. Burnham's continued reliance on the classics and the perceived failure to break new ground until his death might not have been an endearing trait to some. Ultimately, if a particular design trend or school of art is dismissed, the embrace of its biggest proponent is difficult to initiate.

Still, one must look closely at his later work such as the magnificent steel-framed Flatiron Building in New York (1902), or as represented here in the following pages by his Pennsylvania Station in Pittsburgh (1903) and his Union Station in Washington (1907), designed as part of a larger urban plan. These individual buildings exemplify various aspects of a life's work that are difficult to ignore.

The Visual Survey

The train stations within the visual survey to follow are arranged chronologically in order of their completion. It is felt that the construction process is almost always a period of design work in progress with revisions, additions, and a re-working of plans. The survey illustrates the eclectic nature of urban train station design around the Western world. There were very few examples built utilizing "pure" architecture—the slavish adherence to well-defined architectural models. Beaux-Arts Neoclassical designs and other revivalist forms that dominate this survey borrowed liberally from architectural styles far afield in their striving toward the monumental. Remember, if you will, the aesthetic defined by Carroll Meeks as you search for your own through line and conclusions regarding the development of the station architect's art.

Take note of how architects sought solutions to the problems faced when creating and honing a new form of structure without precedent. Watch as technological developments give rise to beautiful arched balloon sheds, especially in the UK and Germany. Notice the uneasy relationship that develops between train shed and head house as these structures learn to share the same site. Observe how the head house reigns supreme by the early years of the twentieth century as American railroads de-emphasize the train platform area.

Most important, take a moment to ponder the remarkable ability of each and every station pictured to have somehow been able to survive. Through wars, catastrophic fires, or in many cases calculated neglect, these resilient structures somehow dodged the bullet. Stations such as those in Washington, D.C., and St. Louis, with leaking roofs, missing windows, and weakened foundations, held on with little help from the public they were built to serve. Faced with the indignity of adaptive use as the only option for survival, these structures complied. Every station represented here is still standing. How fortunate we are, for their survival enriches our culture. With that in mind, it is my sincere hope that the reader, in the process of embracing this beautiful and diverse collection of public buildings, will witness in illustrated form a clear, evolving, and often surprising testament to where we as a communal Western culture have been and where we have traveled architecturally.

1846

Amiens Street Station, *now known as* Connolly Station
Dublin, Ireland
William Deane Butler

Generally accepted as the earliest example of Italianate architecture built in the Irish capital, Dublin's Connolly Station was the first of four major stations built around the city's central core. This proud Italian palazzo, built as the origination point for the Drogheda & Dublin Railway, was designed by William Deane Butler. The architect imported this design trend from England, where it was experiencing great popularity.

The station facade consists of three towers separated by matching arcades five bays wide. The larger center tower still serves as a station signpost in this decidedly low-rise city. Originally conceived as a stub-end station, the physical layout of the terminal complex is somewhat unusual, as most arriving train tracks terminate at an angle in relationship to the head house.

Known as Amiens Street Station when completed, the terminal was renamed in 1966 in honor of Irish rebel and patriot James Connolly, who was executed for his participation in the 1916 Easter Uprising, a crucial step in the republic's struggle toward independence.

The early twenty-first century saw the completion of a station remodel confined mostly to platforms, concourse, and south-facing entrance foyer. Remarkably, the main terminal facade appears almost exactly as it did upon completion in 1846. In addition to interurban trains serving Belfast and other cities up and down the east coast of the island, a growing commuter train system now calls on Connolly Station.

Facing page: Connolly Station.

1848

Kingsbridge Station, *now known as* Heuston Station
Dublin, Ireland

Sancton Wood

The Great Southern & Western Railway was the third and largest company to lay track outbound from Dublin during those years of intense railroad construction in the mid-nineteenth century. In retrospect, the company's success is quite surprising. Completion of this railroad to the west and south came at a time when famine and lack of rural opportunity drove ticket sales—usually a one-time, one-way purchase—either to Dublin or to the nearest deep seaport, as Irish men and women fled for the Americas and beyond by the hundreds of thousands. In essence, this particular railroad's inadvertent initial function was to expedite the elimination of potential patrons.

In 1847 the company's route map was fairly complete, but the Dublin terminus was not, having fallen victim to labor unrest and dwindling funds. This classical station, designed by the railroad's own architect, Sancton Wood, was described as a "Renaissance palazzo" upon completion. Dominating the site is a multistory Italianate office block constructed of granite that served as corporate headquarters. The train shed is situated adjacent to the multistory block, but it was not originally attached. The length of the shed is concealed from the street by a Neoclassical block of nine bays framed by Corinthian columns and balustrades that serves as a strong and formal station entrance. In the late 1990s, the entire complex was restored and unified, with tracks and platforms extended to the office block, effectively creating a classic stub-end station.

In Dublin railroad tradition, this terminal was renamed in honor of yet another executed veteran of the 1916 Easter Uprising, 19-year-old Sean Heuston, a one-time railroad employee.

Facing page: Heuston Station booking hall.

Facing page: Office block portion of Heuston Station.

Main entrance.

Principal facade of Gare de l'Est featuring the "expressed arch" lunette window.

1852

Gare de Strasbourg, *now known as* Gare de l'Est
Paris, France
François-Alexandre Duquesney

As architects worked toward a solution to the unique design questions posed by the new phenomenon of passenger rail travel, designer François-Alexandre Duquesney devised a plan that became a model for decades to come. By the mid-nineteenth century, two-sided stations, those which segregated departing passengers on one side of train tracks from arriving passengers on the other, had become quite common. As the cumbersome movement of increasing numbers of passengers began to strangle that generation of stations, Duquesney and engineer Pierre Cabanel de Sermet successfully combined arrival and departure functions in a central structure set at the stub end of multiple train tracks. Construction began in 1847. The head-type station had been born. As a result Gare de l'Est, as it came to be known just two years after completion, was often cited throughout the remainder of the nineteenth century as the finest railway station ever built.

The station's main room or ticketing hall was more an interior street, a glazed-roof arcade providing pedestrian access in a straight line from street to track. The room's facade prominently featured a lunette window that, for the first time on this scale, externally expressed the arched shed behind. This use of an exterior arch motif would become a staple of station architecture lasting well into the twentieth century.

A sizable addition to the east of the station's principal entrance, larger than the original structure in the same Neo-Renaissance style, was completed in 1931. At that time a lateral departure hall was spread across the base of the stub-end tracks.

The station's "interior street" serves as the ticketing hall of Gare de l'Est.

Exterior of Gare de l'Est's current train shed and departure hall roof.

The shed structure as it stands today is unique if not downright curious. A series of extremely shallow conjoined arched sheds extend off the back side of the lateral arched shed of the departure hall just long enough to cover parked locomotives and adjacent platforms. Beyond this point the extending platforms are minimally protected.

The French military repeatedly exploited the station's efficiencies throughout the course of three major wars. Gare de l'Est was a primary debarkation point for troops traveling to "the front." Following World War II, those same efficiencies were mocked and ridiculed by the memory of thousands of Parisian Jews who were loaded onto trains bound for the camps of Eastern Europe. Despite the station's checkered history, the original mid-nineteenth-century portions of this departure point for all points east remain amazingly true to their original appearance.

View of the departure hall, Gare de l'Est, added in the 1930s.

Paddington's shed interior.

1854

Paddington Station
London, England

Isambard Kingdom Brunel and Matthew Digby Wyatt

Designed by Isambard Brunel, chief engineer of the Great Western Railroad, this mammoth ridge-and-furrow cast-iron and glass canopy was clearly influenced by plans for Joseph Paxton's extraordinary Crystal Palace, built in 1850. In fact, Brunel had been a member of the Great Exhibition building committee, which guided construction of the Crystal Palace in London's Hyde Park.

Unlike the other major passenger terminals serving London, Paddington was built without a formal head house or significant entrance facade. The great focus of interest here is specifically the train shed. Originally, three parallel and conjoined arched sheds covered the train platforms with a span of 238 feet. The impressive canopy incorporates two transepts situated midway down the length of the structure. These arched, spatial corridors created a complicated cross design overhead that was a marvel of mid-nineteenth-century British engineering prowess. Cast-iron support columns discreetly disguised downspouts carrying rainwater from the roof to drainage points under the concourse floor. Decorative flourishes were kept to a minimum. Yet iron roof beams were punctured with fanciful star and planet cutouts. Triple fanlights at the concourse end of the shed were decorated with curious swirling Moorish forms, adding whimsy to this massive exercise in strict geometric design. These particular bolt-on details are usually attributed to Matthew Digby Wyatt, the architect responsible for the stodgy office structure within the shed on the terminal's southwest side. A fourth parallel shed spanning an additional 109 feet was added to the terminal between 1906 and 1916.

The Great Western Railway owned the tracks that traveled closest to Windsor Castle, "country home" to the British royal family. Because of this, royals were no strangers to Paddington, often utilizing a private waiting room along track number one. This private space, now a railroad first-class lounge, was also a gathering point for family members in advance of funeral trains departing the station for royal interment at Windsor, most notably Queen Victoria in 1901, King Edward VII in 1910, and George V in 1936.

Extensive station redevelopment completed in 1999 now provides rail passengers with in-shed access to a multitude of goods and services. The bright spot in this renovation can be found in the creative lighting design that emphasizes the station's singular strength: a structural clarity that is both functional and appealing.

One of Paddington's three fanlights with Wyatt's bolt-on Moorish ironwork.

Gare du Nord's principal facade.

1866

Gare du Nord
Paris, France
Jacques Ignace Hittorf

This Paris train station was built to replace an overburdened terminal facility less than fifteen years old. German-born architect Jacques Hittorf designed this admirable effort to unify a station head house and train shed within a single coherent structure as he neared his seventieth birthday.

Construction began in 1861 on the stub-end station, originally built as a shallow U-shaped structure wrapped around a train shed covering eight stub-end tracks and four platforms. Each of the wings parallel to the tracks contained basic passenger services such as waiting rooms and baggage facilities. Rapid passenger growth immediately following the station's completion required additional trackage. The head house structure was deepened along the frontage block to allow the consolidation of the terminal's various facilities. Additional tracks and platforms could then be added laterally into the station wings.

The shed's triangular roof trusses, which were originally of wood, are supported by two rows of thin cast-iron columns and span over 236 feet. Brackets at the tops of these columns help support roof beams and impart a sprightly air to the interior. The shed peaks at an impressive 125 feet. The triangularity of the train shed designed by François Leonce Reynaud is in stark contrast to what was being built elsewhere, especially in Britain, where an arched shed was viewed as aesthetically superior.

The station's main facade is a Neoclassical composition featuring a large glazed triumphal arch flanked by two smaller arches. When the shape of the train shed behind is considered, it is clear that Hittorf's use of the arch at Gare du Nord had progressed from a literal expression of internal function to the role of station signpost. The arch would continue to perform this duty on station facades worldwide. Weighty Ionic pilasters add vertical emphasis to the overall horizontal composition. These vertical motives battle with a practical but unfortunate marquee that was added to the entire length of the building in 1930.

The liberal use of allegorical sculpture, a common device in French station design, foreshadows formal Beaux-Arts style. Placed across the facade are no fewer than twenty-three sculptures representing cities served by this facility, as well as sculptures of ancient gods, all created by a group of the nation's top artists. This intemperate display could only amplify the Second Empire's self-perception of cultural superiority in the mid-nineteenth century.

By 1958 a tired and worn Gare du Nord came close to demolition. Greatly expanded through the years, the station is vital once again, serving French and European cities north of Paris as well as London via Eurostar.

Facing page: Gare du Nord's original peaked train shed.

1874

St. Pancras Station
London, England

Sir George Gilbert Scott

The London terminus of the Midland Railway, St. Pancras Station, was created in two phases: initially the construction of one of the world's first great "balloon-type" train sheds, then a wraparound head house station and hotel of over-the-top Victorian excess.

The magnificent single-span shed of iron and glass, designed by William Henry Barlow and R. M. Ordish, was 240 feet wide, soared 100 feet at its highest point, and ran 689 feet in length. The shed was completed in 1867. Architectural historians often cite the arch used in shed design as the single most important design innovation of the nineteenth century. Surely the completed shed at St. Pancras became the yardstick of success for all arched sheds to follow.

Sir George Gilbert Scott designed an elaborate 500-room hotel and terminal building of Victorian Gothic Revival architecture. Construction began in 1868. This imposing structure, as viewed from the street with its multiple spires towering above a red-orange brick confection coupled with candy cane arches, columns, gables, and gargoyles, is said to have often been mistaken for a cathedral. This confusion no doubt pleased the Midland Railway.

St. Pancras Station was praised upon completion, perhaps reinforcing the commonly held image of a British culture striving for engineering and architectural achievement, with the modern empire speeding forward at the top of its game. However, the twentieth century found architectural critics revising history's view and dismissing the station's importance as a monument to Victorian excess. The most enduring criticism seems to lie in the belief that St. Pancras had little to do with purposeful station design. In an unexpected way, the architect may have been in agreement. In his memoirs, Scott noted, "This work has been spoken of by one of the revilers of my profession with abject contempt. . . . It is often spoken of to me as the finest building in London; my own belief is that it is possibly too good for its purpose" (Meeks, *The Railroad Station*, 96).

The 1990s brought a limited restoration and cleanup of the complex. The critics and historians have warmed once more to the charms of St. Pancras. Regardless of how history remembers this architectural undertaking, one fact remains: well over a century has passed since construction was completed, and this awe-inspiring terminal still possesses the ability to astonish at every turn.

Facing page: The gothic hotel and terminal building of St. Pancras Station.

The arched shed at London's St. Pancras Station.

Facing page: The booking hall at St. Pancras.

1874

Liverpool Street Station
London, England
Edward Wilson

Originally built by the Great Eastern Railway, Liverpool Street Station serves the City of London, Britain's financial heart. Edward Wilson, an engineer, took a difficult site and created a station under a highly refined truss-supported train shed that is both complex and amazingly weightless in appearance. The 278-foot span is supported by a series of paired cast-iron columns smoothly tied to the next pair by arches and often decorated with a lacy fretwork. A concourse transept unifies the series of four conjoined train sheds. The structure's detail draws the eye upward and provides a sense of airiness to the entire space. Over the years, architectural critics have been impressed by the station's original multilevel pedestrian flow, a variation of which still exists today.

Although many stations around the world have been "shopping mauled" during their renewal process, the Liverpool Street Station in its current state is still a very active train terminal. Extensive renovation work undertaken by British Rail in the late 1980s paid unanticipated respect to the old, transforming the station quite effectively for modern passenger service into the new century.

Facing page: The truss-supported train shed floats above the extensive and effective renovation work completed in the 1980s.

An updated entrance to London's Liverpool Street Station.

Central Station's concourse and Jacobean Central Hotel addition.

Facing page: The shed of Glasgow's Central Station.

1879

Central Station
Glasgow, Scotland
Sir Robert Rowand Anderson

Scotland's largest city was at one time served by four railway terminals. When the grand and Gothic St. Enoch Station was leveled in the 1970s, most interurban rail traffic had already been consolidated at Glasgow's Central Station (Walker, *Glasgow*, 74).

Construction of Central Station was viable only after the Caledonian Railway successfully bridged the River Clyde in 1878. The large greenhouse-like shed, with its repeating ridges and valleys, is supported by lattice trusses that traverse the passenger platforms. This visually intricate glass and steel structure was attached to a multistory office structure, all designed by Sir Robert Rowand Anderson. Just five years later, Anderson was contracted again, this time to convert the office building into the Central Hotel. The head house lodging is Edwardian in design, with a curious but pleasing two-story Jacobean addition pushing purposefully onto the concourse floor.

In 1899, as this industrial city prospered, a major station expansion was undertaken, increasing the number of tracks and platforms and expanding the concourse area. The resulting product, designed by Donald A. Matheson and James Miller, was a light-filled urban terminal that was both airy and spacious. The track-side main floor of the hotel served station duties such as ticketing, baggage, and food service.

A redevelopment and restoration project undertaken in the late 1990s saw structural work performed on the complex train shed, including the replacement of all 30,000 pieces of glass that cover a square area of 6.8 acres. Additional food and retail shops were added to serve 90,000 visitors and 500 train movements daily.

1880

Queen Street Station
Glasgow, Scotland

James Carsewell

Situated just off Glasgow's main square, Queen Street Station is not a traditional big-city terminal but rather a simple iron and glass train shed supported by a series of bowstring trusses floating over seven terminating rail lines. This facility specializes in short-haul intercity trains within Scotland and therefore operates efficiently without the need or benefit of a clearly defined formal waiting room or ticketing hall.

Three parallel glazed skylights run the entire length of the shed, offering the gift of additional natural light to an enclosed space in a part of the world not known for sunny skies. The bow roof is partially enclosed on either end with soft fans of hanging opaque glass. The structural clarity of the design is so well honed, one might be hard-pressed to visually ascertain the station's date of construction.

This location was the site of Glasgow's first railroad station, known as Dundas Street Station. That original terminal, built in 1842, was razed to accommodate the construction of Queen Street Station in 1878.

Facing page: Queen Street Station's timeless train shed design.

1885

Polk Street Depot, *later known as* Dearborn Street Station
Chicago, Illinois
Cyrus L. W. Eidlitz

Romanesque Revival design, as popularized by architect H. H. Richardson, was all the rage in the United States in the 1880s and 1890s. The style was characterized by the use of heavy, rough-cut stone, overscaled round arches with turrets, and deeply recessed windows. Those design cues were somewhat softened by New York architect Cyrus L. W. Eidlitz in his design for Polk Street Depot. This terminal building is one of the oldest urban train stations still standing in America. Constructed of red brick on a pink granite base with terra-cotta detailing, the original design was sturdy, functional, and mostly devoid of Victorian excess. However, its current appearance is really the result of renovations following a substantial fire in 1922. A formal addition of a third story was added on either side of the clock tower, where only dormers previously existed. Steeply pitched roof lines were removed, including a spooky Flemish-inspired A-frame roof atop the twelve-story tower.

This head-end station was the smallest of the six major terminals serving Chicago well into the twentieth century. With its shortened passenger platforms and a congested train yard constricted by an overpass and multiple street crossings, this most inefficient of urban stations served as home to seven of the city's twenty passenger railroads as America entered World War II. Perhaps most notably, the Santa Fe Railroad offered travelers the promise of a modern, streamlined escape to the exotic landscapes of the desert Southwest. That daily westbound journey began at what was by then known as Dearborn Street Station.

Although Dearborn Street was decommissioned in 1971, like so many American stations following the formation of Amtrak, the terminal had already served Chicago passengers continuously for eighty-six years. In the 1980s, the vacant structure was restored, and its interior spaces were converted to office and retail use. The train yard was cleared for a residential community of apartments and townhouses. The station now serves as the centerpiece of a vibrant, reemerging neighborhood just south of Chicago's Loop.

Facing page: The Romanesque Revival architecture of Dearborn Street Station, representative of many built in that style in the 1880s.

The five conjoined sheds at Frankfurt's main station peek from
behind the massive frontage block.

1888

Centralbahnhof, *now known as* Hauptbahnhof
Frankfurt-am-Main
Germany
Georg P. H. Eggert

This enormous railroad station has always been notable for its sheer size. But the station is also noteworthy for its visual symbolism: an architectural and engineering expression of a new nation and expanding empire. In 1879, after the relatively quick defeat of Napoleon III in the Franco-Prussian War, construction began on an unusual type of union station at Frankfurt-am-Main. The terminal's three original conjoined sheds, each 183 feet wide and 610 feet long, were to represent three of the many distinct regions unified under the new German Empire and newly served at this single location. Although the glazed spans appear as perfect arcs, Johann Schwedler's shed design utilizes tapered ribs that begin at track level and come to an almost indiscernible point 93 feet above the tracks. From the street, these pleasing forms appear to peek from behind the station's 689-foot-long frontage clad in German Palatinate and Heilbronner sandstones.

The facade of Georg P. H. Eggert's main pavilion pushes forward from the principal elevation. The requisite monumental station arch sports a lunette window over three arched entrance doors. Flanking the arch are embellished turrets, while above is a 20-foot-high bronze allegorical sculpture of figures representing steam and electricity and the Greek god Atlas as he struggles to carry the weight of the world. Just inside is the station's original booking hall, with a 75-foot-high vaulted ceiling that mimics and continues the lines of the shed's central span visible beyond.

Placed between the large and rambling head house and the colossal glazed train shed was an oversized lateral concourse perpendicular to the terminal's eighteen stub-end tracks. Built larger

One of the Hauptbahnhof's smaller train sheds added in the 1920s.

37

Facing page: The monumental arch of the station's main entrance.

The five conjoined sheds set against the high-rise backdrop of modern-day Frankfurt.

than seemingly necessary for peak passenger use, it appears to have been designed for major troop movement as well. This concourse, one of the first of its kind, had exits to the street on both ends that negated the arriving passengers' need to travel through the head house bottleneck. This minor refinement of foot traffic flow was a revelation for a station this size.

As originally built, the station building was a U-shaped structure situated around the stub-end tracks. In 1912 the two return wings that served administrative duties were removed; they were replaced twelve years later with two train sheds, one on each side of the original trio.

Frankfurt's Hauptbahnhof, the largest in Europe for more than twenty-five years, did not endure World War II unscathed. Amazingly, it was not until March 1944 that tracks leading into the complex were hit by Allied bombs. Portions of the massive multi-span shed and the south wing (to the left of the main entrance) sustained damage as well. Full restoration was not undertaken until the 1950s.

Frankfurt's Hauptbahnhof clearly and outwardly expresses its function from blocks away in a loud and declarative way. What once served 187 daily trains when it first opened now handles 1,100 intercity trains, 700 commuter trains, and 350,000 visitors daily.

A total restoration of the station's shed is scheduled for completion in 2006, with a price tag of well over US$100 million.

The eclectic Orientalist style of Istanbul's Sirkeci Station.

1890

Musir Hamdi Pasa, *now known as* Sirkeci Station
Istanbul, Turkey
A. Jasmund

Following Turkey's involvement in the Crimean War, the city of Istanbul began a gradual journey toward westernization as train service arrived from Europe. Musir Hamdi Pasa was built primarily to receive the Orient Express in a grand manner. In fact, Sultan Abdülaziz was quite enthusiastic in accommodating the arrival of this new link. He personally approved the laying of track through the grounds of Topkapi Palace, destroying gardens and ancient walls, thereby allowing quick construction of a worthy railway terminal on the banks of the Bosporus.

The new terminal was built in an exotic and rather eclectic Orientalist style. A. Jasmund's design incorporated Eastern motifs, colored tile work, and two rather pleasing minaret clock towers that stand in mosque-like contrast to the station's bulky main structure. Originally each tower was topped with a pear-shaped dome approximately one-fourth the height of the entire tower. Modern amenities included gas lighting and heating throughout, utilizing stoves imported from Austria. The station was situated on a gradual slope below the palace just steps from the sea. Gardens originally surrounded the station and provided a park-like welcome for arriving passengers. As the city grew, this green belt disappeared.

During the late 1950s and early 1960s, the station restaurant served as a hangout for the local literati. Now known as Sirkeci Station, the terminal is still an active rail depot. The Orient Express discontinued service to Istanbul in 1977.

The waiting room at Sirkeci Station.

41

1894

Union Station
St. Louis, Missouri

Theodore C. Link and Edward D. Cameron

Toward the end of the nineteenth century, the city of St. Louis was quickly establishing itself as a primary transfer point for rail passengers traveling across the broad landscape of North America. An overworked terminal built here in 1870 desperately needed replacing. German-born St. Louis resident Theodore C. Link was awarded the commission and a $10,000 prize to design what was to be at the time of completion the largest terminal complex in the world. Link was partnered with architect Edward D. Cameron, a former employee of Romanesque Revival maven H. H. Richardson. Link and Cameron parted ways just before construction began in 1891.

Looking somewhat like a medieval castle, the head house appears to lean back from the street in an attempt to balance an astonishing clock tower with its bulging bartizan rising 230 feet. The tower and principal facades are clad in a rough-hewn light-colored limestone. Deep and heavy Romanesque arches intermingle with Norman gables and exterior detailing. A steep triangulated roof of gray Spanish tile was replaced with red tile in 1955.

Entering the head house from the street, the departing passenger could climb a short flight of stairs to the terminal's Grand Hall, one of the most elegant interior spaces constructed in conjunction with train travel. The architects reinterpreted the conventional

Facing page: The head house of Union Station blends Romanesque and Norman Revival styles in this medieval castle.

Union Station in St. Louis.

use of the barrel vault, 65 feet at its highest point, by reducing the height of the supporting side walls. Romanesque arches softened with decorative plaster work puncture the perimeter of the room. The result is a placid space that envelops the visitor. Adjoining this stunning public space was a seventy-room hotel and a Harvey House restaurant. Assembled together one story down at track level were multiple waiting rooms, ticketing offices, a lunch room, and a post office.

Head house decor attributed to Louis Millet features the use of extensive decorative plaster and frescos, gilt surfaces, faux marble, and stained glass panels. A massive chandelier in the Grand Hall that incorporated hundreds of individual bulbs was donated to a scrap metal drive during World War II. Other decorative lighting fixtures have survived, most notably the haunting sculptures of the female form.

The train shed designed by George H. Pegram was originally 606 feet wide and stretched 630 feet down the length of the thirty-two stub-end tracks. This mammoth structure, with its tin-covered wooden roof, was lengthened further to 810 feet on the eve of the 1903 St. Louis World's Fair. Although the shed's exterior worked aesthetically within the realm of Link's picturesque composition, the interior disappoints. A pleasing shallow curve defines the upper cord of the shed's arch, but the interior view is obscured by five spans utilizing Pegram's patented but visually bewildering railroad bridge truss. Ultimately this immense structure fails to engage by virtue of its overwhelming scale.

In its heyday, Union Station served 22 trunk railroads, accommodated 270 long-distance trains daily, and hosted 22 million passengers annually. By the time America's national passenger railroad was formed in 1971, only six trains called on St. Louis daily. Amtrak would leave the station for good in 1978, and the entire complex would be quietly shuttered.

An exacting head house restoration and shed adaptive use project were completed in 1985 at a cost of more than $135 million. Union Station is once again the most visited tourist site in St. Louis.

Daniel Burnham's remarkable exterior "carriage concourse" of steel and terra-cotta.

1903

Union Station, *later known as* Pennsylvania Station
Pittsburgh, Pennsylvania
Daniel H. Burnham

The turn of the century saw the rise of a new wrinkle in American train station design—the station as office building. In 1898, Daniel H. Burnham began designing his take on the trend for the mighty Pennsylvania Railroad. This Pittsburgh station site was geographically restrictive, at first inhibiting the architect's more flamboyant leanings. The completed terminal, the third to be built at this location, comprised three major elements. The complex was centered by a twelve-story office block of rather straightforward design. Behind this early high-rise was the last great balloon shed built in America, a glass and steel span stretching 240 feet over platforms and tracks and running 550 feet in length. This shed was unique in its ability to expand and contract on metal rollers in response to Pittsburgh's somewhat severe climate. An inspired addition to the plan was a truly outrageous and quite beautiful exterior rotunda placed in front of the office building as a covered carriage concourse. The walls of the circular space were hung from a steel frame and clad in terra-cotta. A round skylight of opaque glass offered filtered natural light. The space was adorned with French pendentives bearing the names of the railroad's major cities of service.

Passenger train service is still available in Pittsburgh via an adjacent site. The twelve-story station building and rotunda are now elements of an up-market apartment complex. The mammoth train shed was demolished in 1947.

The train station as office building in Pittsburgh, one of several examples built in the United States.

47

1903

Broad Street Station
Newark, New Jersey

Frank J. Nies

The Lackawanna Railroad (Delaware, Lackawanna & Western) was flush with cash. Coal was king, and the railroad's freight operation had a lock on many of the anthracite coalfields of eastern Pennsylvania. New railroad president William Haynes Truesdale undertook a major rebuilding project along the Lackawanna's main line from the Hudson River on New York's harbor through Pennsylvania to the city of Buffalo. Special attention was given to northern New Jersey, an area of prime industrial real estate and home to some of America's toniest suburbs. Truesdale was intent on the electrification of the railroad's developing commuter train operation, while eliminating twenty-seven cumbersome grade crossings.

As the main line tracks were elevated, work began on a new brick and limestone through station to serve the growing city of Newark. In-house designer Frank J. Nies created a three-story Renaissance Revival structure that features an 80-foot-high campanile faced with clocks mounted within decorative scrollwork. Parading limestone arches frame some of the oversized windows. Two hipped roof dormers dominate the station's street side.

Passengers can still enter the station at the base of the clock tower and climb a flight of stairs to the mezzanine, originally home to the ticket office and coffee shop. Here, interior walls are lined with dark bricks coated with an uneven white glaze. Square support columns are topped with repeating plaster emblems sporting the original railroad monogram. Eastbound passengers must climb an additional story to the third floor and a rather plain waiting room at track level. Westbound passengers move through a pedestrian passage under the elevated tracks, then up to a separate waiting room adjacent to the platforms three stories above street level.

As the 1960s came to an end, so did long-distance passenger service at Broad Street Station. However, much of the Lackawanna's commuter service survives intact, operated now by New Jersey Transit. Presently the station's exterior is virtually restored, but NJT, an ongoing champion of station preservation, has contributed heavily to the added $60 million earmarked for the century-old terminal. In addition to extensive work required to make the facility handicap-compliant, interior restoration and renovation plus extensive platform work will be completed for the benefit of passengers connecting with hundreds of commuter trains each business day.

Facing page: Broad Street Station in Newark, New Jersey.

1903

Galveston, Harrisburg & San Antonio Station, *later known as* Southern Pacific Depot
San Antonio, Texas

J. D. Isaacs and Daniel J. Patterson

The station built originally for the Galveston, Harrisburg & San Antonio Railroad is most notable for its highly developed sense of place. As the Beaux-Arts movement began to take root, architects J. D. Isaacs and Daniel J. Patterson bucked the developing trend by designing a Mission Revival depot with Baroque detailing, appropriate for this Texas city, which continues to embrace a strong cultural influence from south of the border. The terminal facade is reminiscent of the iconic Alamo, located just blocks away in the city's downtown.

The station waiting room is vaulted, the ceiling coffered and replete with skylight and elaborate plaster detailing. A grand wooden staircase rises from the station floor to offices located off matching second-floor balconies. On the room's south wall above the staircase is a stained glass window featuring the "lone star" Texas state seal.

Southern Pacific Depot was partially restored in the 1980s, and then a major restoration and adaptive use project were undertaken in 1998. A missing stained glass window from the building's main elevation was re-created to match the original specs. Active train station duties were moved several hundred feet to the south into a newly built structure of a similar style.

Facing page: The Galveston, Harrisburg & San Antonio Station interior and preserved "lone star" stained glass window.

The Mission Revival facade of the station.

51

1906

Bush shed

Hoboken, New Jersey

Lincoln Bush

Throughout the history of train station design, specific architectural styles and trends would rise and fall in popularity. However, it was primarily a practical consideration that changed the overall look of the large station complex in North America at the beginning of the twentieth century.

In 1904 Lincoln Bush, the chief engineer of the Delaware, Lackawanna & Western Railroad, devised a radical yet practical alternative to costly balloon-type train sheds. The modular Bush shed was a simple span supported from the center of a passenger platform across two tracks to a support point at the center of the next adjacent platform. Spans were simply bolted together down the length of the station's platforms and across adjacent track pairs. Constructed of steel, reinforced concrete, copper, and glass, the Bush shed provided slots positioned inches above the smokestacks of steam locomotives as a means of venting smoke and soot from the platform environment. The very first Bush shed, installed in 1906 and pictured here at Lackawanna Terminal, originally incorporated the extensive use of glazed skylights above the actual platforms and between the two exhaust slots. As the years ticked by, the practical aspects of Bush's creation were honed even further. By 1914, twelve important train stations across the United States and Canada included the use of the patented low-cost shed. Later versions completely eliminated the structural steel framing, as fabrication depended solely on the use of reinforced concrete. As railroads sought to control costs and maximize profits, aesthetic focus shifted to the station head house. The magic and beauty of a well-designed shed would quickly be forgotten and would not be revisited again until the era of European railroad reinvention beginning in the 1990s.

Facing page: The first Bush shed, built in Hoboken, New Jersey, has been somewhat altered from its original form.

Union Station in Washington, D.C.

1907

Union Station

Washington, D.C.

Daniel H. Burnham

Architect Daniel H. Burnham was initially engaged to orchestrate the Washington Plan, an urban design for the U.S. capital that would provide focus and a degree of grandness akin to the great cities of Europe. While in Rome with members of the U.S. Senate Park Commission, he began to sketch what was to become Union Station, based on the ancient baths of the emperor Diocletian. The urban plan would take years to actualize, but Burnham's sketch for a new monumental train station was immediately appealing to Pennsylvania Railroad president Alexander Cassatt.

Work began in 1903 on this Beaux-Arts terminal of great grace and grandeur. The station was a textbook stub-end design serving seven railroads. One entered the edifice through one of three archways flanked with requisite limestone columns. Just inside was a barrel-vaulted waiting room running 220 by 130 feet. The ceiling reached 93 feet at its highest point. Burnham expressed this barrel vault on the exterior of the structure as well.

To the left was the ticketing and baggage alcove, separated from the waiting room by a peristyle providing a platform for eight of the many draped statues found throughout the structure. During construction, the terminal's board of directors ordered ceremonial battle shields placed strategically in front of these sculptures in an attempt to conceal their masculinity.

To the right of the waiting room was the Savarin Restaurant, a fine dining establishment with a frosted glass skylight, famous for its raw oyster bar and popular with the city's carriage trade. Directly behind the waiting room through a three-bay central portico of white Vermont granite was the vaulted passenger concourse. This 760-foot-long space was said at the time of completion to be the largest room of any kind in the world. Passengers would traverse the 130-foot width to the train platforms just beyond.

Like most cities in the United States, Washington saw a precipitous drop in railroad passengers in the years following World War II. Although the city was located on the southern end of the relatively healthy Northeast (rail) corridor, diminishing passenger loads may have appeared more conspicuous here when considering the grand scale of the station.

In the 1970s, the massive roof began leaking, and chunks of ceiling plaster fell. A halfhearted cleanup and city visitor center conversion in 1976 were ill-conceived. After $48 million was spent on the project, politicians and other public officials went to great lengths to distance themselves from any involvement. By 1981, Union Station was boarded shut. Passenger trains still utilized some of the original platforms, but patrons were diverted to the street through a Byzantine network of makeshift plywood passages. The end seemed very near indeed.

In 1981, Congress passed the Union Station Redevelopment Act, clearing the way for a massive adaptive use project that took five years and $160 million to complete. A meticulously detailed restoration was proudly presented to the public when the doors of the station complex opened once again in 1988. Retail and dining are scattered throughout all areas of the terminal building.

One can always bemoan the use of such a historic station site for a major retail operation. Nevertheless, the quality of the restoration work, coupled with economic realities, may soften one's outrage. Union Station is still a functioning train station that might not have endured without the infusion of mixed-use dollars.

Entrance to the station's original waiting room.

The barrel vault of the ticketing and baggage alcove.

1907

Lackawanna Terminal

Hoboken, New Jersey

Kenneth M. Murchison

As railroads approached New York City from the south and west, those companies were confronted with the challenge of transporting passengers and goods across the formidable Hudson River to the island of Manhattan. At one time as many as five combination train/ferry depots lined New Jersey's side of the river. Perhaps none was as successful in execution as the terminal designed by New York architect Kenneth M. Murchison for the Delaware, Lackawanna & Western Railroad.

This proud Beaux-Arts terminal featured a head house with late French Baroque detailing and was tied to a two-story ferry terminal at a 120-degree angle. As many as six ferries could dock at once, with passengers boarding the boats on level two, while cargo wagons and trucks entered from the ground floor. The DL&W provided ferry service from this train station to three waterfront locations within the city of New York.

Completed in 1907, Lackawanna Terminal was the fifth station built at this specific site, this time on a concrete platform partially over water and supported by wooden pylons. Rusticated Indiana limestone was utilized on the ground-level exterior surfaces. Because of settlement concerns coupled with the physical impact of arriving ferries, Murchison devised a clever solution to the inevitable cracks that would form on the upper reaches of the building facade. He designed copper-clad, iron-reinforced panels that were bolted to the building's exterior masonry. The original 225-foot-high clock tower, since dismantled, was also clad in copper. The resulting look was a stunning complement to the riverfront. It is difficult to imagine the visual impact of this newly built intermodal complex, heavily lit at night, with its preoxidized copper-glow serving as an unreal beacon on New York's western horizon.

The waiting room of Lackawanna Terminal is approximately 100 feet square, with a 50-foot-high ceiling and a stained glass skylight. Heavy brass chandeliers with opaque globes were hung near the four corners of the room. Limestone covers the interior walls to window height. Elegant ornamental ironwork is utilized in healthy doses.

Ferry service to Manhattan ceased in the late 1960s. Long-distance passenger service ended in 1970. The terminal facility has survived due to heavy commuter rail traffic on former Lackawanna Railroad lines. New Jersey Transit has orchestrated a $300 million restoration of Lackawanna Terminal.

Facing page: The copper-clad Lackawanna Terminal in Hoboken, New Jersey.

The waiting room at
Lackawanna Terminal.

1908

Delaware, Lackawanna & Western Station, *also known as* Lackawanna Station

Scranton, Pennsylvania

Kenneth M. Murchison

Much of the wealth of the Lackawanna Railroad was attributable to the transport of anthracite coal. The city of Scranton sat in the midst of this wellspring and was rewarded for its good fortune in 1908 as the railroad completed construction of a rather grand terminal in the center of this small but prosperous burg.

Architect Kenneth M. Murchison, having recently designed the Lackawanna's Hoboken terminal, was awarded design duties as a result of a limited competition held in 1907. His winning entry was a five-story French Renaissance depot complete with a mansard roof. When construction began, a more reserved Neoclassical structure evolved, stripped of its Beaux-Arts bluster. The station is clad in Indiana limestone and topped with a large clock flanked by sculpted eagles. Above the main entrance, six Doric columns rise three stories above a wraparound marquee, and engaged pilasters of equal height are repeated around the remainder of the building. A sixth floor providing additional office space was added to the structure in 1923.

The main waiting room, two and a half stories in height, is lined with Sienna and Alpine green marble and complemented with overscaled brass lighting fixtures. This space was capped with a barrel-vaulted ceiling of leaded glass. Around the perimeter of the space above eye level are thirty-six faience panels based on paintings by Clark G. Voorhees depicting scenes found along the railroad's right-of-way. This extravagant station jewel built for a city of this size truly reflects the prosperity enjoyed by the Lackawanna Railroad in the late nineteenth and early twentieth centuries. Yet

Facing page: The waiting room interior of Lackawanna Station.

The Lackawanna Railroad's station in Scranton, Pennsylvania.

it is still surprising to learn that construction was undertaken to accommodate only twelve passenger trains a day.

Service to Scranton ended in January 1970. The railroad declared bankruptcy two years later. After a decade of neglect, the structure emerged as a hotel following a $13 million restoration in 1983.

1909

Franz Josef Nadrazi, *now known as* Hlavni Nadrazi

Prague, Czech Republic

Josef Fanta

By the early twentieth century, Prague was home to a dazzling display of Art Nouveau design referred to regionally as Secese (modern style). This romantic design trend was an assimilation of motifs from nature, such as plant life, with those adopted from local folk architecture. The proliferation of Secese architecture was advanced by a small group of middle-aged designers including Josef Fanta, the architect responsible for the city's Franz Josef Station. Prototypically, Secese architecture encompassed the use of undulating curves almost anywhere within a particular set of blueprints, from a building's overall exterior outline, in stylized floral ornamentation, to more practical applications such as detailing on stair railings, protective marquees, and lighting fixtures. By the time Prague's principal train station was completed after nine years of construction, the free-flowing look of early Secese architecture had given way to a more restrained geometrical form.

The brick and plaster facade of this station features a glazed arch over the original main entryway. The entrance is protected by an iron and glass marquee. Two substantial towers flank the arch and morph from a square form to a more cylindrical shape as the towers rise and project above the roof line. Disconcerting glazed spheres cap these towers. Two expansive multistory stepped wings stretch out in either direction from the main structure and culminate in sizable matching office blocks. The northern wing, originally home to the station's restaurant space, contains well-preserved ceramic scenes in classic Art Nouveau/Secese style. Exuberant allegorical sculptures flank the entrance arch, while additional works are displayed just inside a semispherical space that originally served as the booking hall.

Throughout most of the 1970s, Hlavni Nadrazi was disrupted by a prolonged and insensitive addition project. A partially submerged booking hall in a then-modern "eastern bloc" style was placed below and in front of the existing terminal under a stretch of limited-access highway. Ticketing and other passenger services were confined to this rambling, poorly lit, and dreary bunker, while much of the original station complex sat empty above ground. Plans for total renovation and adaptive use were drawn up, but they still await financing and approval.

Facing page: The Art Nouveau–inspired facade of
Hlavni Nadrazi in Prague.

1911

Hovedbannegård
Copenhagen, Denmark

Heinrich E. C. Wenck

The Danish national railway's chief architect, Heinrich E. C. Wenck, had begun work on the capital's new central station while still smarting from strong criticism of his 1894 nationalistic station design for nearby Østerport. With a modest exterior of terra-cotta brick, a triangulated roof over the main entrance vestibule, underscaled medieval turrets, and pinnacles topped with copper detailing, the design for Copenhagen's Hovedbannegård is a softened albeit castle-like example of Danish national romanticism. A curious use of exterior stone veneer work creates the illusion of columns seemingly borrowed from a child's storybook, yet this helps define porticos used sporadically around the building's perimeter. Inside, sixteen intricate iron chandeliers once contributed to the station's warm baronial air.

This midsize through station, which took five years to complete, was originally noteworthy for its functionality. In a sly nod to traditional station design, Wenck's main passenger hall resembles a finely crafted double-span train shed of brick and timber that served as both a concourse and a waiting room. The architect orchestrated an effective yet unobtrusive segregation of departing and arriving passengers within this largest interior volume. The station's platforms, submerged beneath the head house, were specifically designated for either passenger use or baggage-handling duties.

A thorough renovation project completed in 1994 unified the main hall of this important rail hub with the addition of an undistinguished linear retail strip in the center of the space. Hard surfaces throughout the station complex were renewed, and new custom lighting was added. Lighting designer Gunver Hansen felt strongly about restoring one of the original iron chandeliers, which had been removed from the station in the 1960s and installed in other railroad facilities throughout the country. Ironically, Wenck's controversial Østerport station contained four of these hefty fixtures, and a trade was arranged. Two of these noble chandeliers now hang proudly in their original home.

Although Copenhagen's Hovedbannegård is the principal interurban train station in Denmark, it is not the busiest. The Nørreport commuter rail and subway station, located just blocks away, consistently tops the nation's passenger tally.

Facing page: The passenger hall at Copenhagen's principal station.

Exterior portico, Hovedbannegård, Copenhagen.

Facing page: One of the original station chandeliers back in place after a thirty-year absence.

1911

Union Station, *now known as* Pennsylvania Station
Baltimore, Maryland

Kenneth M. Murchison

Union Station in Baltimore was designed by Beaux-Arts practitioner Kenneth M. Murchison, an architect with an impressive list of completed train station designs. Renamed Pennsylvania Station in 1928, it has an exterior clad in pink Milford granite and is an enlarged and simple reworking of the architect's earlier Neoclassical design in Scranton, Pennsylvania.

This particular commission excels in the success of its serene and intimate waiting room, only 95 feet in length. The room's pleasing proportions are complemented by Sicilian and Pentelic marbles, which cover the interior surfaces. Doric columns support a second-story balcony. Two original mahogany benches with integrated candelabras have survived the years. The entire two-story space is bathed in a warm glow from three stained glass skylights that were painted over during World War II as an air-raid precaution. The beauty of the tinted natural light was hidden from public view until the 1980s. A pale terrazzo floor provides a rather muted backdrop for this almost spiritual interior space on America's busy Northeast Corridor.

Facing page: Waiting room interior, Baltimore.

Grand Central Terminal, New York City.

1913

Grand Central Terminal
New York City

Reed & Stem with Warren & Wetmore

In 1903, the New York Central Railroad, controlled by the Vanderbilt family, held a two-month competition for a new Grand Central Terminal to replace an opulent French Empire station of the same name. The Minnesota firm of Reed & Stem was awarded the design duties. Charles Reed was the brother-in-law of the New York Central's chief civil engineer. The new design called for a Beaux-Arts jewel to be placed in the center of New York's Park Avenue, diverting the street around the building's perimeter in a "circumferential plaza." The exterior facade of Stony Creek granite and Bedford limestone was designed by the collaborating firm of Warren & Wetmore.

The station concourse, now a familiar American icon, is a large public room 375 by 125 feet. Despite these dimensions, the space feels quite intimate. The pale flooring of Tennessee marble is lightened further by trios of arched windows. In the center of the concourse, an information booth is anchored by the famous four-faced station clock in highly polished brass. The vaulted ceiling 120 feet above depicts the Mediterranean night sky with painted and backlit stars. Zodiac figures are outlined in gold.

The original waiting room, now a special events space called the Vanderbilt Ballroom, is clad in a simulated Caen limestone and finished with a Botticino marble wainscoting. Illumination is provided by five ornate bare-bulb bronze chandeliers in an inverted umbrella shape suspended from the ceiling 63 feet above.

Original bare-bulb chandeliers light the way to a lower departure level.

As the United States entered World War II, Grand Central's 67 underground tracks accommodated roughly 600 trains and 110,000 passengers on a daily basis. Presently, the station is the New York terminus for an extensive system of electrified commuter rail lines serving the northern reaches of metropolitan New York City. These heavily utilized routes survive those originally operated by the New York Central and New Haven railroads many years earlier.

A $187 million restoration and renovation project, completed in 1998, was undertaken to create a rail hub fit for the new century. Poor interior additions of past years were stripped away. The concourse "star ceiling" was restored to its original splendor, utilizing fiber-optic technology. Additional shops have been added along various corridors, providing an unobtrusive retail environment. The underutilized lower concourse has become a food court with New York's celebrated Oyster Bar restaurant as the centerpiece.

"No better station of its size has ever been built," declared historian Carroll Meeks in 1956. Indeed, the city of New York has firmly embraced this beautiful terminal. The emotional connection, although due in no small part to the station's architectural success, may have roots in a silent acknowledgment of a city's shortsighted ambivalence toward the late, magnificent Pennsylvania Station, unceremoniously leveled just across town in 1963.

The concourse at Grand Central.

Facing page: The terminal's original waiting room, now a special events space called the Vanderbilt Ballroom.

1914

Vancouver Station
Vancouver, Canada

Barott, Blackadar & Webster

The railroads of Canada replaced many of their larger stations in the early twentieth century, turning a blind eye to the wonderful châteauesque architectural style of the previous generation. That earlier trend, still visible in a few of the country's surviving railroad hotels, blends Scottish baronial design, and its rough-hewn stonework, turrets, and dormers, with that of the medieval French châteaux and its use of steep mansard roofs fabricated in sheets of copper. The resulting blend, although having much in common with Romanesque Revival architecture, seemed inherently Canadian in nature as it mirrored French and Scottish influences that helped form the early national character.

Work began in 1912 on the Canadian Pacific Railroad's Vancouver Station. Designed by the prominent Montreal-based firm of Barott, Blackadar & Webster, this Neoclassical station features a heavy white Ionic colonnade set against a red brick office block. The building's main elevation is somewhat reminiscent of New York's Pennsylvania Station of 1910. In fact, team architect Ernest Isbell Barott, an American by birth, practiced architecture at Penn Station design firm McKim, Mead & White before moving to Canada in 1911.

The principal interior space, the waiting room, is enveloped by additional Ionic columns and pilasters supporting a frieze of landscape oil paintings depicting the railroad's right-of-way from Vancouver on the coast, then east through the Rockies to Calgary on the Canadian prairie.

The Canadian Pacific of the early twentieth century was not only a railroad company but also the owner and operator of a substantial fleet of steamships that plied the waters of the world. Vancouver Station's site adjacent to the city's bay front allowed for passenger and freight interconnectivity. By 1978, with the company's long-distance rail service just a memory, the building was converted to office space, with the main floor interior adapted for retail use. Echoing earlier duties, the station building currently serves as a portal to a ferry depot with vessels to the city's northern suburbs. Also, a fledgling commuter rail line originating at the terminal began service through the city's eastern suburbs in 1995.

Facing page, top: The principal elevation of Vancouver Station.

Facing page, bottom: Landscape oil paintings share space with decorative frieze work near the ceiling of the station's waiting room.

Santa Fe Depot's waiting room and ticketing hall shared space with this art installation in the 1990s.

Facing page: San Diego's Santa Fe Depot.

1915

Union Depot, *later known as* Santa Fe Depot
San Diego, California
John R. Bakewell and Arthur Brown Jr.

San Diego's Union Depot was built as a portal to the city's Panama-California Exposition of 1915–16 commemorating the opening of the Panama Canal. The new station building replaced an 1887 Victorian depot just across the tracks. Design duties were handled by John R. Bakewell and Arthur Brown Jr., the architects responsible for San Francisco's Beaux-Arts jewel, the Civic Center.

Constructed by the Atchison, Topeka & Santa Fe Railroad for $300,000, the 605-foot-long steel-framed, stucco-clad structure was topped with a red tile roof. The main entrance features a monumental archway flanked by twin Moorish towers topped with domes tiled in a zigzag design. Inside the waiting room, a series of arches propel the eye along the 170-foot length of the room. A ceiling of redwood along with sixteen bronze chandeliers and oak benches add warmth to this cool and airy space. In 1949 the railroad replaced the original bifacial clock on the waiting room's south window wall with a corporate Santa Fe medallion.

Following the depot's placement on the National Register of Historic Landmarks in 1972, the property underwent a partial refurbishing. In an attempt to unify the station's waiting room following the removal of the original ticket counter, additional wainscoting of Moorish-style art tile was locally fabricated for the newly exposed surfaces. This wall covering is capped eight and a half feet above the floor with a coordinating frieze in an American Southwest design.

The original forecourt patio, located directly in front of the station and enclosed by an open arcade, was replaced by a parking lot in 1954. A landscaped patio evoking the memory of this feature was created in the early 1990s.

The sporadic restoration work of the 1980s and 1990s, although serviceable, was never wholehearted. Yet this fully functioning railroad station in San Diego is one of the best examples of station Mission Revival architecture still in existence.

1915

Estación Retiro
Buenos Aires, Argentina
Lauriston Condor

Argentina's complicated relationship with England in the twentieth century is footnoted by the construction and location of Retiro Station in Buenos Aires. This Neoclassical stub-end terminal was designed by British architect Lauriston Condor at a time when all twelve railroads in Argentina were owned by the British. Directly in front of the station was the English Tower, which served as a signpost and station clock and was built on the Plaza Britanica with British funds. The plaza and tower were renamed immediately after the end of the mortifying Falklands War.

Exaggerated in its proportions, Retiro's booking hall is a monumental space, 200 by 60 feet, ornamented by a balcony 30 feet above floor level. A vaulted ceiling dome soars 65 feet from the station floor. The adjacent Grand Hall stretches 480 feet. These spaces were decorated with mosaic floor tiles and a 7-foot-high Royal Doulton perimeter faience imported from Britain. The original station sheds were huge; two roofs span 328 feet wide, 82 feet high, and 820 feet long. By world standards, the sheer scale of this station was impressive. Yet the grandeur within is masked by the station's facade, one of a multiple of overlapping railroad frontages on this city square. The building's singularity is difficult to read from the street, distinguished only by the squat and squarish dome surmounting the structure.

A visit to Retiro before its refurbishing in the late 1990s was like a distilled visit to the city of Buenos Aires itself. The station, grand at every turn, was worn around the edges in a sad and heavy-hearted way.

Facing page: The booking hall of Retiro Station, built at a time when all railroads in Argentina were British-owned.

Retiro's Grand Hall.

A monumental arch dominates the facade of Eliel Saarinen's
station in Helsinki.

1919

Rautatieasema
Helsinki, Finland

Eliel Saarinen

By the 1890s, Finnish architects had advanced their regional variant of Art Nouveau, referred to as "modern romanticism." Designers in this style, reminiscent of the English Arts and Crafts movement, drew from the structures found throughout the Finnish countryside while rejecting the mass-produced and emphasizing quality workmanship. Locally accessible building materials such as granite and wood timbers were often used in construction.

In 1904 architect Eliel Saarinen, an important modern romanticist, won the design competition for a major train terminal and office building to replace an obsolete two-track facility. Fellow competitors derided the young architect's winning entry as sentimental, provincial, and not modern enough for the purpose of train transportation. Perhaps the design community desired a more mainstream architectural statement befitting the capitals of Europe farther south. Saarinen was determined to deliver a pleasing solution. He and his wife immediately undertook a tour of the great terminals of Britain and Germany in order to alter his plans for Helsinki's new railway station.

Although construction began quickly on the railroad's four-story office building, construction would not begin on the actual stub-end terminal building until 1910. The completed composition of pink granite was an asymmetrical design of clean lines incorporating a station-defining gateway arch framed with decorative copper and underscored by a copper marquee. Flanking the main entrance are two sets of sculpture, matching guardians of massive proportions attributed to artist Emil Wikström. These expressionless giants holding illuminating globes threaten to upstage Saarinen's completed composition. Yet their emotional repose coupled with their inherent strength and detailing finds these doormen strangely comforting as they silently promise to protect the approaching visitor.

An expressive clock tower rises approximately 160 feet. Its complex octagon form is sheathed in rising planes of granite block before reaching a four-faced clock and faceted dome. As a spatial volume, this tower served as a useful device for the architect in controlling the picturesque meanderings of this rather large station complex.

New developments in the use of concrete allowed Saarinen to create a series of undulating arches in the original waiting room and matching station restaurant. The architect's movement away from his original and much hardier modern romantic design saw the elimination of most figurative ornamental detail. Instead, he incorporated geometric decoration into structural elements that expressed the architecture itself. His finished design of stark functional form, sometimes described as a later example of Finnish Art Nouveau, moves headlong toward the coming Art Deco movement, yet maintains a somewhat heavy and quite definite Scandinavian feel.

The structure was virtually completed by 1914, but the demands of World War I found it pressed into service not as a railroad station but as a Russian military hospital. The terminal was dedicated to passenger train service in March 1919, although some interior decor details were yet to be finished.

Rautatieasema's octagonal clock tower.

Giant sculpted guardians protect the station's main entrance.

In 1923, Saarinen and his family emigrated to the United States, where he continued to work. His Finnish-born son Eero rose to prominence for his modern architectural statements, most notably the TWA terminal at New York's Kennedy Airport and the sleek and soaring Gateway Arch along the Mississippi riverfront in St. Louis.

The booking hall interior with its geometric decoration.

Richmond's Union Station.

1919

Union Station, *also known as* Broad Street Station

Richmond, Virginia

John Russell Pope

The clean lines of this Beaux-Arts Neoclassical station were supplied by New York architect John Russell Pope. His limestone-clad terminal features a Doric-columned portico with a coffered ceiling guarding the main entrance and a 105-foot-high dome that caps the marble and limestone waiting room. Pope was also responsible for designing the Jefferson Memorial in Washington, D.C.

Problematic grade crossings in the city of Richmond, coupled with insufficient rail capacity, necessitated the construction of a new terminal with tracks lower than the main structure. An enclosed "gallery" was laid perpendicular above the tracks on the backside of the station. This space served as an additional waiting room. Passengers could quickly connect to the platforms below by staircases, ensuring a speedy departure. Station architecture often embraced this specific design solution—for example, in Baltimore in 1910, followed by the massive Union Station in Kansas City circa 1913.

Although passenger loads waned in the 1950s, the Virginia Museum of Fine Arts named Broad Street Station one of the twelve best buildings in Virginia. By the mid-1970s, the terminal was slated for demolition, but it was rescued to serve as a new home for the Science Museum of Virginia.

Interior of Union Station.

Station waiting room and ticketing hall of the Jacksonville Union Terminal.

Facing page: Jacksonville's Union Terminal.

1919

Jacksonville Union Terminal
Jacksonville, Florida

Kenneth M. Murchison

The scale of this Beaux-Arts Neoclassical station might seem too large for Jacksonville, yet reflects that city's early role as the gateway to a newly emerging vacationland and host to four major railroads. At the time of the station's completion, the city was actually the second largest in the state. Union Terminal was Florida's busiest, serving two hundred trains a day.

As one approached the terminal in its heyday, the pale limestone-clad reinforced concrete structure glowed in the Florida sunshine. A classic colonnade composed of fourteen solid limestone columns, 42 feet high, greeted the departing passengers. Inside, the barrel-vaulted waiting room, which also served as a booking hall, rose 75 feet above a marble floor. Today this monochrome space feels cool yet filled with light. Architect Kenneth M. Murchison was nearing the end of his station design oeuvre. Completing the work he began in Hoboken and Scranton, his design in the Beaux-Arts vernacular was stripped of the unnecessary, leaving only the clean and straightforward while making a rather heroic statement.

Jacksonville's Union Terminal found new life in 1986 as the centerpiece of the city's convention center.

Toronto's Union Station entrance colonnade.

1920

Union Station
Toronto, Canada

George A. Ross, Robert H. MacDonald, Hugh G. Jones, and John M. Lyle

Construction began in 1914 on the third Union Station to be built in Toronto. Canada's two major railroads, the Grand Trunk Railroad (soon to become the Canadian National) and the Canadian Pacific Railroad, joined forces to erect what some refer to as the only Canadian challenger to the greatest of the Beaux-Arts stations ever built. Undertaken on a site close to the city's lakefront, the new facility would solve grade separation issues while promising additional train and passenger capacity for the city. Although the terminal building was virtually complete by 1920, it was not opened for service until 1927 due to a protracted political squabble between the city and the railroads over the requisite track viaduct work.

The station's frontage, stretching over 750 feet, is dominated by a central entrance colonnade of twenty-two Doric columns of Bedford limestone, reminiscent of the ancient Greek temple at Delos. Inspiration for the Grand Concourse, which also serves as a ticket lobby, was drawn from the Roman baths of Caracalla and features a curving coffered ceiling of vitrified Gustavino tiles 88 feet in height at its highest point. The walls of this 250-foot-long public room (once the largest enclosed space in Canada) are covered with "Zumbro stone" from Missouri. Tennessee marble in gray and pink covers the floor in a framed herringbone pattern. At the east and west ends of the space, 40-foot arched window units with integrated doorways are framed by coffered barrel vaults inspired by the Basilica of Constantine. On the north and south walls, inscribed halfway to the ceiling, are the names of the twenty-seven principal cities served by the two original railroads. The use of classical statuary was scheduled for placement throughout the facility but was never realized. Trains of this through station were accessed by a depressed concourse running under the slightly elevated tracks. Passenger platforms were protected by Bush train sheds 1,200 feet long.

Toronto's Union Station was not immune to the precipitous drop in passenger rail traffic following World War II. Its existence was threatened several times, especially in the 1960s. Public and corporate funds were gathered for a C$3 million cleanup of the terminal. In 1965 the government of Ontario announced the creation of commuter "GO" train service, from Union Station as a hub to the far suburbs of Toronto along the shores of Lake Ontario. In subsequent years this service has been greatly expanded in many directions and serves to sustain the vitality of a terminal that handles 120,000 visitors daily and minimal long-distance passenger service.

Union Station in Toronto has not survived without detractors. The main facade of this classic Beaux-Arts terminal building has been criticized by some as too repetitious and cold. With the rise of Canadian nationalism in the second half of the twentieth century, some might argue that this architectural undertaking was simply too derivative of those designs completed years earlier south of the border. Yet, while standing in the Grand Concourse today, caressed by the hushed and echoing footsteps of fellow visitors with eyes drawn in awe to the soaring shadowy heights of the station's coffered ceiling, one appreciates this building's undeniable power to transport and alter a traveler's mood.

Toronto's Union Station.

Facing page: The Grand Concourse.

Chicago's Union Station.

1925

Union Station
Chicago, Illinois

Graham, Anderson, Probst & White

If there ever was a "railroad town" in the late nineteenth and early twentieth centuries, Chicago certainly fit the bill. Twenty trunk railroads served the city. Due to geography, industrial might, and a burgeoning population, the "City of Big Shoulders" served as one of America's primary distribution hubs for both goods and passengers. With this chore came many major railroad terminal buildings spread around the edge of the city's core, following a more European model of station placement.

Design work on Union Station was interrupted in 1912 by the death of Chicago-based Daniel H. Burnham. The firm of Graham, Anderson, Probst & White, the successor to D. H. Burnham & Co., assumed the project and revised the design, with construction commencing in 1914. A world war, material shortages, and labor strife further delayed completion of this impressive terminal until 1925.

The station's principal structure is a classical Beaux-Arts building of Indiana limestone that fills a city block and is fronted by a colonnade which rivaled that of New York's late Penn Station. Rising over the terminal is an eight-story office block, punctured by a massive air shaft that allows natural light to filter into the waiting room below.

From inside, an opaque skylight stretches from wall to wall, floating above a pink Tennessee marble floor. A layer of World War II blackout paint was removed to reveal the natural light in the 1980s. The room of rose, cream, and gold tones was modeled after the ancient Roman baths of Caracalla and features ornate columns and brass torchieres decorated with flora and fauna. This building, containing the grand waiting room, plus ticketing, baggage, and other service functions, was joined by a broad underground passage to a free-standing concourse building of Neoclassical proportions that was demolished in 1969.

A respectful restoration project was undertaken in the early 1990s, giving a fresh face to this grande dame as she labors on, proudly serving a struggling national railroad.

Chicago Union Station's grand waiting room.

Facing page: The ornate columns and torchieres of the station's waiting room.

1928

Hauptbahnhof
Stuttgart, Germany

Paul Bonatz and Friedrich E. Scholer

This satisfying main station complex in Stuttgart has been trivialized, perhaps for having too strong a sense of place. Indeed, at first glance, the slightly foreboding structure may feel Teutonic in nature, and by extension, as has been suggested, prescient of a coming Fascist storm. But this finely crafted station is really another kind of preview, a display of the early strains of the coming Modernist movement. Classical architecture has been stripped here of much of its detailing. Rather plain rectangular volumes have been assembled together to strike a balance. The arrival portico on the main elevation plus the use of the symbolic train station arch and the rough surfaces of the exterior limestone cladding are certainly remnants of the past, but this proud train terminal looks clearly to the future.

Architects Paul Bonatz and Friedrich E. Scholer designed a U-shaped station utilizing new steel and concrete framing technology set around the elevated stub-end tracks. A sizable cross platform separates tracks from the major enclosed space, a lengthy concourse lit by a phalanx of semicircular windows within parading bays running down the length of the room.

The principal facade is marked by two arched entrances separated by a simplified portico. The east entrance, closest to the stark 184-foot clock tower, leads to a sizable vestibule and a wide staircase with access to the second floor concourse and platforms. The west entrance features a semi-enclosed staircase leading to an intimate second-story booking hall adjacent to the concourse. This lovely room, which no longer serves its original function, is decorated with subtle masonry work of brick and smooth stone in a near-Moorish manner.

Original construction of the station was interrupted by World War I and the financial crisis that followed. In 1944 the station was utterly devastated by Allied bombing; it was virtually rebuilt between 1947 and 1960. The original iron and wood train sheds have been replaced with a series of Bush-like sheds fabricated of white opaque glass. Plans are under way to submerge both tracks and platforms to accommodate high-speed through trains while freeing valuable land within the city's center.

Facing page: The "Teutonic" facade of Stuttgart's Hauptbahnhof.

Stuttgart's second-floor concourse.

The former booking hall.

1930

Railway Station

Auckland, New Zealand

Gummer & Ford

This Neoclassical terminal building constructed on re-claimed land near Auckland's harbor is every bit as American in tone and demeanor as the best of the Beaux-Arts terminal buildings in the United States. It was the work of Gummer & Ford, New Zealand's preeminent commercial architecture firm at the time. William Henry Gummer was most likely responsible for the bulk of the design work. While in training he spent much of 1911 in England working with Sir Edwin Lutyens, one of the United Kingdom's leading architects, who was fascinated with the emergence of classicism in design. This internship was followed by a brief stint in Chicago with D. H. Burnham & Co. Following a lengthy career in his native New Zealand, William Gummer is best remembered for his interpretation of a spare form of Neoclassicism.

Located near Auckland's center, this terminal building possesses a clearly defined form while utilizing finely realized brickwork, marble Corinthian interior columns, English Arts and Crafts tile work, and a touch of Art Deco in the terrazzo floor surfaces.

The scale of the Auckland station project coupled with its cost was unheard of in New Zealand at the time. The New Zealand Institute of Architects awarded Gummer & Ford a gold medal for the design in 1931. The structure was converted in 1999 for use as student housing. Tracks and platforms behind the station building continue to provide limited passenger rail service.

Facing page: The Railway Station in Auckland.

The original waiting room of the Auckland Railway Station.

Decorative logo tile.

1933

Pennsylvania Station, *now known as* Thirtieth Street Station
Philadelphia, Pennsylvania
Graham, Anderson, Probst & White

At the dawn of the twentieth century, the Philadelphia-based Pennsylvania Railroad found itself in the enviable position of being the world's largest. At its height the company employed close to 280,000 people, with 5,000 train movements daily. Although the company already had an appropriately scaled hometown terminal in the mammoth Broad Street Station, that aging stub-end facility was encumbered by urban geography and the inability to efficiently serve through trains to and from New York.

The Chicago design firm of Graham, Anderson, Probst & White was hired to create a new terminal on the west side of the city's downtown. The railroad had worked with this company several years earlier as one of the principal players in the construction of Union Station in Chicago. "The Pennsy" had a taste for the grandiose and knew what this design team was capable of creating. Construction began in 1929.

The terminal complex as completed might be described as severe, yet the design shows hints of an evolving American train station vernacular, as Beaux-Arts Neoclassicism gives heed to the warming influence of Art Deco. The exterior's east and west facades feature impressive porticos of 71-foot Corinthian columns fashioned from Alabama limestone. Inside, the station's concourse is 290 feet long, 135 feet wide, and 95 feet high. A coffered ceiling of red, cream, and gold presides over Roman travertine walls and a Tennessee marble floor. Ten 18-foot-long Art Deco lighting fixtures hang from the ceiling like so many drop earrings.

Following an area-wide rail electrification program, the entire station was placed directly over active train tracks. The possibility of smoke and soot seeping into the station's interior would no longer be a concern. Passengers move downstairs to catch intercity trains and upstairs on the north side of the terminal to tracks servicing suburban trains. This excellent plan for passenger movement within the building has generally been praised, yet comments like "uninspired Mausoleum" (Meeks, *The Railroad Station*, 133) and "flashy grandiosity" (Richards, *The Railway Station*, 47) haunt the station's legacy. Regardless, it is difficult to deny the station's sense of absolute scale and stately presence.

Thirtieth Street Station, America's largest surviving passenger station, was placed on the National Register of Historic Places in 1978. Amtrak has spent tens of millions of dollars on restoration, and a limited mixed-use project was completed in the 1990s.

Facing page: The western facade of Thirtieth Street Station.

The 290-foot station concourse in Philadelphia.

Facing page: The massive Corinthian columns in the station concourse.

The dramatic entrance arch of Cincinnati's Union Terminal.

1933

Cincinnati Union Terminal
Cincinnati, Ohio

Fellheimer & Wagner with Roland Wank and Paul Philippe Cret

I n the 1920s, this hilly Midwestern city on the banks of the Ohio River was host to seven trunk railroads utilizing five terminal facilities, all prone to seasonal flooding. Yet competition between the various companies made the idea of a true union station on higher ground difficult to advance. Finally, in 1929, site preparation for a joint terminal began on a plot one mile northwest of the downtown core. Although not centrally located, the elevated site allowed for a quarter-mile-long landscaped visual link to the city's center featuring a cascading water feature and one of the best vantage points of downtown Cincinnati, which exists to this day.

The New York architectural firm of Fellheimer & Wagner first developed a conservative Neoclassical design scheme that was deemed too costly and too staid by the partnered railroads guiding the project. Hungarian architect Roland Wank and French designer Paul Philippe Cret, both graduates of the École des Beaux-Arts, were brought in to rework the plans.

The main structure of the complex, a monumental semispherical dome clad in limestone and marble, sits on a man-made rise. The dramatic entrance arch, 200 feet in diameter, features a series of vertical window columns. Centered on the facade between two limestone pylons is a 16-foot-wide clock with hands of red neon—the only touch of color found anywhere on the main elevation. A sizable marquee trimmed in black granite with an aluminum band punctuates the entranceway. Curved low wings stretch out from

Detailing within the great rotunda.

111

From the floor of Cincinnati Union Terminal's rotunda, one of the glass mosaic murals by Winold Reiss.

either side of the main building mass. This imposing monochromatic exterior belies the visual riot awaiting inside.

Curves and swirls of color greet the visitor upon arrival within the half dome's interior. The acoustic plaster ceiling of this ticketing rotunda in shades of golden umber, burnt sienna, and silver is suspended from an unexposed series of structural arches spanning a space of 125 by 176 feet. The ceiling of this impressive space soars 106 feet. An information kiosk sits center stage on circular pathways of colored terrazzo. Eighteen ticket windows are positioned around the curved perimeter of the space.

Dominating the rotunda are two large glass mosaic murals by German émigré Winold Reiss. These vibrant works, each more than 20 feet high by 125 feet in length, wrap around the back wall of the semisphere. The south mural depicts the history of American transportation; the north mural illustrates scenes of Cincinnati's development. A host of other station services and vendors, such as restaurants and a newsreel theater, could originally be found around the rotunda periphery. The use of rich surface materials throughout the terminal, such as red Verona and black Virginia marbles, local Rookwood Pottery tiles, chrome, and exotic woods, appears to contradict the clients' cost-saving directives.

A mammoth rectangular concourse and waiting room, dismantled in the 1970s, originally extended from the rear of the rotunda. That staggering space, 78 by 410 feet, was positioned over

The plaster ceiling of the station's semispherical dome.

the terminal's fourteen tracks and eight passenger platforms. A softly vaulted ceiling capped the room, and fourteen Reiss mosaics depicting Cincinnati industries covered most of the wall space. Many of these vibrant works in glass survive to this day at the city's airport.

The design team responsible for Cincinnati's new Union Terminal was able to blend fashionable Art Deco design cues with the formality of Neoclassicism in a work that was both strong and welcoming. It would seem that a fresh and fluent architectural dialect had been developed that was well suited to train station functions. Yet the terminal was built for a future America that was never meant to be. Although the terminal's capacity was occasion-

ally taxed during World War II, the nation's passenger volume had already begun a steep downward spiral by opening day in 1933.

In 1986, with the demolition of the remaining terminal structures seemingly inevitable, $44 million in public funds was earmarked for adaptive use, renovation, and restoration. Original underground parking and ramp space were utilized to create the Cincinnati Museum Center at Union Terminal, now home to three city museums. First opened in 1990, this sensitive use of terminal space has allowed the noble facade and resplendent rotunda to remain nearly intact. Amtrak returned in 1991.

1935

Pennsylvania Station
Newark, New Jersey
McKim, Mead & White

McKim, Mead & White, the architectural firm responsible for New York's late, great Pennsylvania Station circa 1910, was approached by the city of Newark and the Pennsylvania Railroad to create a truly intermodal transportation center for New Jersey's largest city. Although much smaller in scale, this Pennsylvania Station, completed in the depths of the Great Depression, is a head-turner—an overlooked jewel that would have made the design firm's founders truly proud.

In the late 1920s, the railroad and the city of Newark agreed to share in the undertaking of a $42 million plan to combine most transportation modes serving Newark within a single complex. Long-distance trains of the Pennsylvania Railroad as well as electrified commuter trains of the area would be elevated above ground level, with tracks and platforms placed literally on top of a large portion of the new terminal. Elsewhere on three levels, space was dedicated for underground trains to New York as well as bus, trolley, and automobile interconnectivity. In addition, Newark's underground streetcar line, developed in conjunction with the WPA, was incorporated into the terminal development.

The exterior facade, clad in Indiana limestone, has a decidedly horizontal feel and features a parade of pilasters that frame repeating grids of aluminum windows. Few station designs provide for so much natural interior light. Arched portals of rubbed pink granite

Facing page: Under Pennsylvania Station's entrance marquee.

Newark's Pennsylvania Station.

puncture the facade, their curvature accented by Art Deco rosettes carved in stone. An aluminum marquee protects each entrance to the terminal. The underside of the main marquee features a sunburst design surrounded by a series of metallic concentric circles decorated with swirling metal stars and white lightbulbs. The razor-sharp roof line is interrupted by another Art Deco motif that serves as a background for a Modernist clock face replete with concealed backlighting.

The main waiting room is a stately and symmetrical space, deriving attention from its simplicity and surprising use of color. This sizable room running 175 by 58 feet utilizes a red terrazzo floor with brass banding and inlays of black and yellow. A high wainscoting of rose-yellow Montana travertine encircles the entire waiting area. Thirteen raised plaster medallions are evenly spaced along the perimeter walls, depicting various modes of transportation.

The flattened arched ceiling is a deep sky blue, with undulating gold leaf patterns. Parading down the center of the space and hanging from 46 feet above are a series of 800-pound Art Deco lighting fixtures. These globes of flashed opal glass are banded with white bronze and decorated with the signs of the zodiac. Passenger benches of rich gray walnut include aluminum accents.

When Pennsylvania Station opened its doors to the traveling public in 1935, this unexpected architectural display tipped its hat to the Beaux-Arts of the immediate past while embracing a modern classicism and the Art Deco references in vogue at the time. A major restoration took place in the 1980s, with additional touchups added in the mid-1990s by New Jersey Transit. Seemingly ignored by architectural critics, perhaps by virtue of its location, Newark's Pennsylvania Station is still an active long-distance and commuter rail center.

One of the repeating grids of aluminum windows on Pennsylvania Station's facade.

Facing page: The main waiting room in Newark.

1935

Stazione di Santa Maria Novella

Florence, Italy

Giovanni Michelucci with Pier Niccolo Berardi,
Nello Baroni, Italo Gamberini, Baldassarre Guarnieri,
and Leonardo Lusanna

This strong Modernist statement in the center of a city that serves as a living museum of Renaissance art is quite a surprise. An earlier Romanesque plan by a government in-house architect, Angiolo Mazzoni, was ultimately rejected by the municipal board of Florence for conflicting aesthetically with the church of Santa Maria Novella nearby. As a result, a nationwide competition for a new station plan was orchestrated in 1932. The commission was awarded to a team of Italian Rationalists known as the Tuscan Group (Gruppo Toscano). The winning design was actually a student reworking of a university thesis by Italo Gamberini and supervised by their professor, Giovanni Michelucci.

The completed station, placed on the highest corner of a plaza, is a spare and low rectangular volume running over 525 feet and faced with a local red sandstone. The facade is marked by seven parallel bands of raised stonework. Projecting from the left side of the facade is a low cantilevered canopy that serves as a covered auto entrance. Rising up and over this carport, then rising up again over the station's higher main volume, are seven parallel rivers of opaque glass that the design team dubbed the "glass cascade." This vertical element provides punch to the anonymous station frontage. This same glazing creates the ceiling of the entrance hall just inside the station's main doors and visually guides the passenger traffic flow toward the cross platform and the waiting trains. The use of diffused natural light illuminates simple rooms constructed of rich indigenous marbles and stone.

The finished composition created controversy. Many felt Modernism had no place in the city of Florence. Others felt the station was not monumental enough. In addition, the memory of Professor Michelucci's architectural work in general was somewhat tarnished after World War II by his involvement in several high-profile commissions officially sanctioned by Italy's Fascist government under Mussolini. But the architect would live to see the station in Florence confirmed as one of the most significant Rationalist compositions built, as well as a turning point in Italian architecture. Michelucci died just days before his 100th birthday in 1991.

Facing page: The entrance hall of the Santa Maria Novella Station and the "glass cascade" that forms much of the ceiling.

The concourse in Florence and the overhead river of glass that
guides passengers to departing trains.

The original station restaurant.

The Union Passenger Terminal in Los Angeles.

1939

Union Passenger Terminal, *also known as* Union Station
Los Angeles, California

John and Donald Parkinson with H. L. Gilman, J. H. Christie, and R. J. Wirth

The Los Angeles Union Passenger Terminal, which opened for business in 1939, is generally accepted as the last great railroad station built in America. A new Los Angeles station might have been built much earlier in time and in a different form had it not been for a long and contentious battle between the city and the railroads.

In 1900, Los Angeles had a population of 102,000. By 1930 that figure would balloon to 1.2 million. The city fathers were desperate to embrace their new status as a major American city. As early as 1915, the notion of a world-class railroad terminal was certainly part of that developing civic pride. The three major railroads serving Los Angeles at the time had already established large stations around the downtown area, but the city's growth had encircled these facilities. Many trains were required to travel the length of active city streets to reach their destination. The city wanted the railroads to cooperate in the construction of a union station north of the downtown core as part of a proposed civic center. The railroads resisted, and a battle ensued lasting sixteen years. Finally, in 1931, the U.S. Supreme Court ruled that the California Railroad Commission could legally order the Southern Pacific, Santa Fe, and Union Pacific railroads to build a joint station on the site prescribed by the city. Construction finally began in 1934.

Designed by a team of in-house architects from the three participating railroads, in concert with father-and-son team John and Donald Parkinson, this $13 million terminal complex was a curious yet successful architectural blend of Spanish Colonial Revival, Moorish, and Art Deco design elements. The station embraces the

region's original Spanish heritage, given the use of stucco arcades, patios, balconies, and a belfry. But the various interior spaces give way to modern layout principles while utilizing Moorish and Art Deco detailing. Towering arched windows of diffused glass line two of the four sides of the noble ticketing hall. The beamed

The Harvey House restaurant closed in the 1960s.

Polished marbles dominate Union Passenger Terminal's ticketing hall.

ceiling is painted to simulate wood. The wainscoting is of a three-foot-high geometric design created in art tile by Gladding, McBean & Co., then raised higher with a grid of polished travertine squares. An Art Deco ticket counter of American black walnut runs 115 feet down the length of the room. The interior walls in both the ticketing hall and the main waiting room were covered in a newly developed, neutral-colored acoustical tile incorporating ground corncobs in an attempt to dampen "station echo" during public address system announcements. The floors are polished red quarry tile, interrupted by designs of colored marble. Both rooms share a series of Art Deco–inspired chandeliers, each 10 feet in diameter and weighing 3,000 pounds. The waiting room features an array of oversized Deco armchairs upholstered in leather.

Wherever the Santa Fe Railroad chose to hang its hat, the Fred Harvey Company was sure to follow with one of its signature restaurants. The version here was a stellar space created by Harvey Company in-house designer Mary Colter. The restaurant, closed in the 1960s, is tied to the main station building by an arcade.

The main waiting room and the original armchairs upholstered in leather.

The arched restaurant interior features Moorish plaster work and light fixtures. A large U-shaped lunch counter anchors the room. Tall decorative panels of California art tile serve as a backdrop for tooled leather booths along opposite walls. The flooring incorporates an Art Deco geometric pattern in cement tile.

The modern-day visitor to the station is immediately embraced by the structure's inner glow. The surface finishes and darker color palette provide a cool respite from the glare of the California sun. Yet light reflects everywhere, from the highly polished floors to the painted ceilings and the slick lines of the waiting room armchairs. The tone is never somber, but rather hushed, and yes, maybe somewhat melancholy. These grand rooms of Los Angeles Union Station encourage that protracted farewell, the extension of that good-bye kiss, perhaps for just a moment longer. This last great station in America fits the bill.

In addition to long-distance rail service, the terminal currently serves as the center point of a developing system of commuter rail and citywide rapid transit.

The booking pavilion at Rome's Termini Station.

1951

Stazione Termini
Rome, Italy

Angiolo Mazzoni / Eugenio Montuori with Castellazzi, Fadigati, Vitellozzi & Pintonello

Benito Mussolini himself expressed a desire to replace Rome's central railway station, which had been built in the 1870s. A 1931 design competition was won by Angiolo Mazzoni. Construction began in 1938 on a Rationalist design for a new station that reflected Il Duce's vision of a new Italy. By the time the Fascist government unraveled in 1943, only the two rather lengthy Modern wings with classical references had been completed along the sides of the stub-end tracks. By war's end, the existing plans for the station head house and frontage were tainted by the dead dictator's vision, and a new competition was held.

The architects involved in this second phase of Termini Station were presented with the very real challenge of completing a work in progress while avoiding the historic walls of Aggere Serviano, which are inconveniently located practically in the center of the site. The keynote of their solution was a pronounced entrance and booking pavilion, set off-center within the frontage elevation, featuring a transparent facade of glass and steel. The design team, in consort with engineer Leo Calini, utilized the upper outline of the ancient wall as inspiration for the undulating roof line. The swooping S-curve of reinforced concrete with an exaggerated curbside overhang creates a very real feel of a large outdoor room. A shirttail fascia frieze sculpted by Amerigo Tot provides detailing. Inside, a pale and dreamy color palette of soft iridescent mosaic ceiling tile and pale pink granite flooring creates a calming public space. A curtain wall provides visual access to the geological site, blending the ancient and the modern rather handily.

Set between the pavilion and the stub-end tracks is a monolithic

One of the two wings completed during the early years of World War II is visible from the station's cross platform.

The historic walls of Aggere Serviano are visible at the far end of the booking pavilion in Rome's Termini Station.

office block laid laterally across the site, running 760 feet in length and only 35 feet in depth. The facade is pierced with horizontal window bands that provide controlled natural light at floor and ceiling levels on most floors of the multistory office building. This two-to-a-floor window configuration tends to distort the building's true size. The ground floor of this structure contains station shops and services that open to a large and strikingly simple arcade located just behind.

A series of soft vaults featuring glass brick creates a cross plat-

form ceiling that suggests the great iron sheds of the past. But the struggle between train shed and head house has long since passed. It is here in Rome that engineer and architect had finally worked in tandem, sitting side by side to create something more. The finished station complex, although not completely successful, is a rather remarkable construction that speaks with a truly modern vocabulary. Unbeknownst to its creative team upon completion, Rome's Termini Station would stand unchallenged as the last great station built in Europe for more than forty years.

Bibliography

Bean, Audrey, Michael Fish, Jean-Claude Marsan, Peter Lanken, William Naftel, and Martin Weil. *Windsor Station/La Gare Windsor*. Montreal: Friends of Windsor Station, 1973.

Binney, Marcus. *Great Railway Stations of Europe*. London: Thames and Hudson, 1984.

Binney, Marcus, and David Pearce. *Railway Architecture*. London: Orbis, 1979

Bradley, Bill. *The Last of the Great Stations: Fifty Years of the Los Angeles Union Passenger Terminal*. Marceline, Mo.: Walsworth, 1992.

Brochmann, Odd. *Copenhagen: A History of the City Told through Its Buildings*. Copenhagen: Arkitektens Forlag, 1970.

Brown, Ron. *The Train Doesn't Stop Here Anymore*. Peterborough, Ont.: Broadview Press, 1991.

Condit, Carl W. *The Railroad and the City: A Technological and Urbanistic History of Cincinnati*. Columbus: Ohio State University Press, 1977.

Craig, Maurice James. *Architecture in Ireland*. Dublin: Department of Foreign Affairs, 1978.

Dethier, Jean. *All Stations: A Journey through 150 Years of Railway History*. London: Thames and Hudson, 1981.

Diehl, Lorraine B. *The Late, Great Pennsylvania Station*. New York: American Heritage Press, 1985. Reprint, New York: Four Walls Eight Windows, 1996.

Doordan, Dennis P. *Building Modern Italy: Italian Architecture, 1914–1936*. New York: Princeton Architectural Press, 1988.

Etlin, Richard A. *Modernism in Italian Architecture, 1890–1940*. Cambridge, Mass.: MIT Press, 1991.

Graby, John, and Deirdre O'Connor. *Dublin*. London: Phaidon Press, 1993.

Grant, H. Roger. *Erie-Lackawanna: Death of an American Railroad, 1938–1992*. Stanford, Calif.: Stanford University Press, 1994.

Halberstadt, Hans, and April Halberstadt. *The American Train Depot & Roundhouse*. Osceola, Wis.: Motorbooks International, 1995.

Highsmith, Carol M., and Ted Landphair. *Union Station: A Decorative History of Washington's Grand Terminal*. Washington, D.C.: Chelsea, 1988.

Hines, Thomas. *Burnham of Chicago, Architect and Planner*. New York: Oxford University Press, 1974.

Holland, Kevin J. *Classic American Railroad Terminals*. Osceola, Wis.: MBI, 2001.

Kalman, Harold. *A Concise History of Canadian Architecture*. Oxford: Oxford University Press, 2000.

Lincoln, Colm. *Dublin as a Work of Art*. Dublin: O'Brien Press, 1992.

Meeks, Carroll L. V. *The Railroad Station: An Architectural History*. New Haven, Conn.: Yale University Press, 1956. Reprint, New York: Dover, 1995.

Middleton, William D. *Grand Central, the World's Greatest Railway Terminal*. San Marino, Calif.: Golden West Books, 1977.

Muschamp, Herbert. 1996. "Grand Central as a Hearth in the Heart of the City." *New York Times*, 4 February, metropolitan edition.

O'Connor, Kevin. *Ironing the Land: The Coming of the Railways to Ireland*. Dublin: Gill & Macmillan, 1999.

Ouroussoff, Nicolai. 1997. "The Grand in Central Is Leaving the Station." *Los Angeles Times*, 6 April, metropolitan edition.

Parissien, Steven. *Station to Station*. London: Phaidon Press, 1997.

Potter, Janet Greenstein. *Great American Railroad Stations*. New York: John Wiley, 1996.

Price, James N. *The Railroad Stations of San Diego County, Then and Now*. San Diego: Price & Sieber, 1989, 1998.

Reed, Henry Hope. *Beaux-Arts Architecture in New York: A Photographic Guide*. New York: Dover, 1988.

Richards, Jeffrey, and John M. MacKenzie. *The Railway Station: A Social History*. Oxford: Oxford University Press, 1986.

Saarinen, Eliel. *Search for Form in Art and Architecture*. Mineola, N.Y.: Dover, 1985.

Saarinen in Finland: Exhibition 15.8–14.10.1984. Translated by Marja Alopaeus, Harald Arnkil, Roger Connah, and Desmond O'Rourke. Helsinki: Museum of Finnish Architecture, 1984.

Schaffer, Kristen. *Daniel H. Burnham, Visionary Architect and Planner*. New York: Rizzoli, 2003.

Scull, Theodore W. *Hoboken's Lackawanna Terminal*. New York: Quadrant Press, 1987.

Sheppard, Charles. *Railway Stations: Masterpieces of Architecture*. London: Bracken Books, 1996.

Smith, G. E. Kidder, AIA. *Italy Builds Its Modern Architecture and Native Inheritance*. New York: Reinhold, 1955.

Solomon, Brian. *Railroad Stations*. New York: Michael Friedman, 1998.

Svacha, Rostislav. *Architecture of New Prague, 1895–1945*. Cambridge, Mass.: MIT Press, 1995.

Temple, Egon. *New Finnish Architecture*. Trans. James C. Palmes. New York: F. A. Praeger, 1968.

Ten Italian Architects: An Exhibition Organized by the L.A. Co. Museum of Art under the Direction of Esther McCoy, Feb. 15–April 2, 1967. Los Angeles: L.A. Co. Museum of Art, 1967.

Walker, Frank Arneil. *Glasgow*. London: Phaidon Press, 1992.

Wilson, Richard Guy. *McKim, Mead & White, Architects*. New York: Rizzoli, 1983.

One of the heroic bas-relief figures on the principal facade at Cincinnati's Union Terminal.

Index

Books in the Railroads Past and Present Series

Landmarks on the Iron Railroad: Two Centuries of North American Railroad Engineering by William D. Middleton

South Shore: The Last Interurban (revised second edition) by William D. Middleton

"Yet there isn't a train I wouldn't take": Railroad Journeys by William D. Middleton

The Pennsylvania Railroad in Indiana by William J. Watt

In the Traces: Railroad Paintings of Ted Rose by Ted Rose

A Sampling of Penn Central: Southern Region on Display by Jerry Taylor

The Lake Shore Electric Railway by Herbert H. Harwood Jr. and Robert S. Korach

The Pennsylvania Railroad at Bay: William Riley McKeen and the Terre Haute and Indianapolis Railroad by Richard T. Wallis

The Bridge at Quebec by William D. Middleton

History of the J. G. Brill Company by Debra Brill

Uncle Sam's Locomotives: The USRA and the Nation's Railroads by Eugene L. Huddleston

Metropolitan Railways: Rapid Transit in America by William D. Middleton

Perfecting the American Steam Locomotive by Parker J. Lamb

From Small Town to Downtown: A History of the Jewett Car Company, 1893–1919 by Lawrence A. Brough and James H. Graebner

Steel Trails of Hawkeyeland: Iowa's Railroad Experience by Don L. Hofsommer

CHRISTOPHER BROWN is a former network television executive and broadcast journalist. He currently works as a television field producer and freelance photographer in Los Angeles.

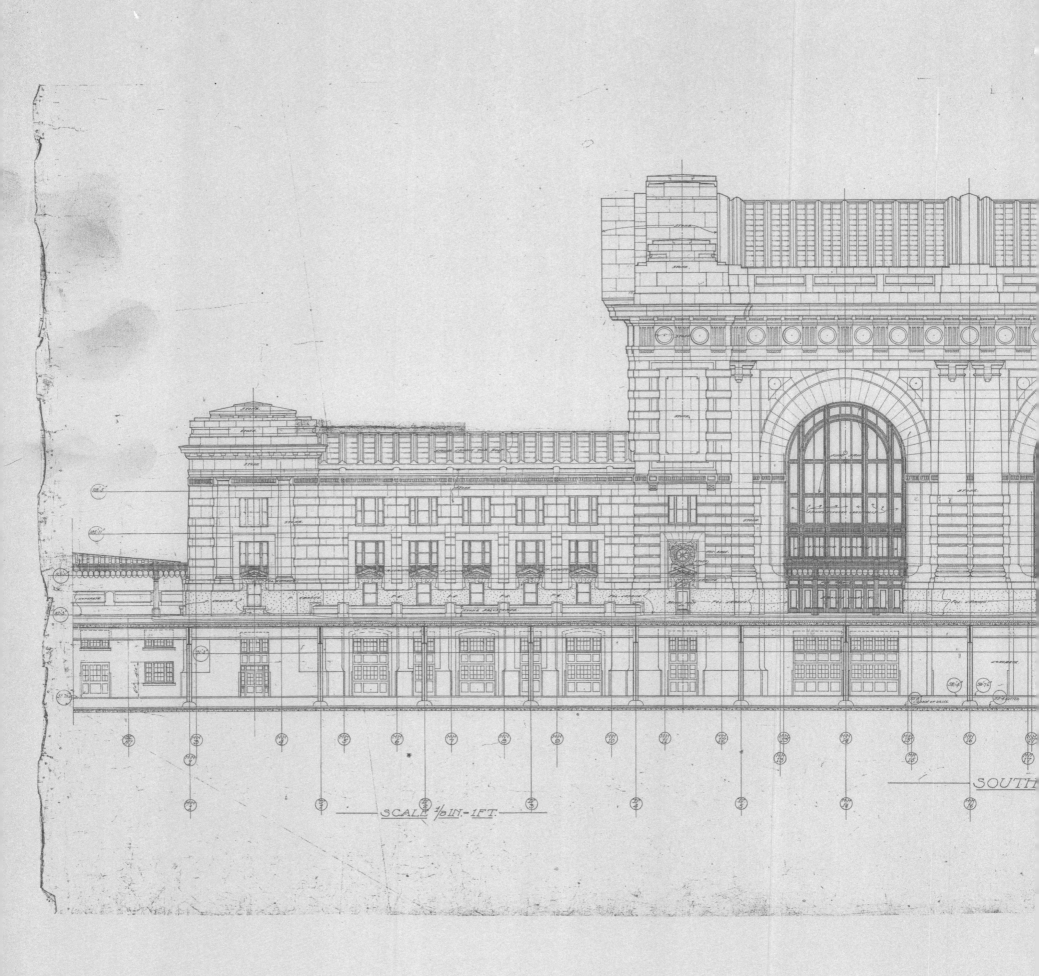

SCALE 1/8 IN.-1FT.

SOUTH